Y0-CCA-271

THE GOSPEL OF THE KINGDOM OF GOD

Heaven's Powerful Influence on Earth

David A. Garcia, Th.D.

THE GOSPEL OF THE KINGDOM OF GOD,
HEAVEN'S POWERFUL INFLUENCE ON EARTH
Copyright © 2016 David Garcia, Th.D.

All rights reserved under International Copyright law. This publication may not be reproduced, stored in a retrieval system, or transmitted in whole or in part, in any form or by any means, electronic, mechanical, photocopying, recording or otherwise, without prior express written permission of the Publisher.

ISBN Number: 978-0-942507-70-6

E-book ISBN Number: 978-0-942507-65-2

Unless otherwise indicated, all Scripture quotations are taken from the New King James Version of the Bible. The Holy Bible, New King James Version. Copyright (c) 1982 by Thomas Nelson, Inc. Used by permission.

Scripture quotations marked (NLT) are taken from the Holy Bible, New Living Translation, copyright © 1996, 2004, 2007 by Tyndale House Foundation. Used by permission of Tyndale House Publishers, Inc., Carol Stream, Illinois 60188. All rights reserved.

Scripture quotations taken from The Message marked (MSG) are copyright © 1993, 1994, 1995, 1996, 2000, 2001, 2002. Used by permission of NavPress Publishing Group.

Scripture quotations marked (AMP) are taken from the Holy Bible: The Amplified Bible. 1987. La Habra, CA: The Lockman Foundation.

In order to maintain consistency, the following words Kingdom, Heaven, and Word (when referring to the Bible) have all been capitalized, even when Bible versions are quoted that normally do not go by this standard.

Address all personal correspondence to:
Pastor David Garcia
Grace World Outreach Church
20366 Cortez Boulevard
Brooksville, FL 34601
Website: www.graceworldag.org

Published by: Deeper Revelation Books
Revealing "the deep things of God" (1 Cor. 2:10)
P.O. Box 4260, Cleveland, TN 37320
Phone: 423-478-2843
Website: www.deeperrevelationbooks.org
Email: info@deeperrevelationbooks.org
Refer to the website for an online catalog of all books published by Deeper Revelation Books, as well as distribution information.

Deeper Revelation Books assists Christian authors in publishing and distributing their books. Final responsibility for design, content, permissions, editorial accuracy, and doctrinal views, either expressed or implied, belong to the author.

Table of Contents

Acknowledgements

I would like to thank my wife, precious Nellie, for her patience, prayers, and support, without which this book would not have been possible. I want to acknowledge the following individuals who also made this book a reality: Bob Armstrong, for your encouragement, editing, and friendship; Mike Shreve, for your insight expertise, editing, and friendship; Luke Kenney, for your excellent book cover design; Gail Cowart, for your typing, copying, and patience with me; To the wonderful people, staff, and leadership at Grace World Outreach Church, Brooksville, FL, whom I love so much; Pat Schatzline, for inspiring me to raise the remnant and think big!

Preface

by Patrick Schatzline

"Are you ready to awaken to a new authority in Christ? Then this book is an absolute must-read for you! It is written for those that are ready to understand what it means to grab ahold of the "keys to the Kingdom" (Matthew 16:19)! When I read The Gospel of the Kingdom, by my very dear friend and mentor, Pastor David Garcia, I was stirred to extreme emotional highs and lows.

The highs that I felt came from understanding that God has not created us to be sitting Christians, which often hatches hypocrites, but rather we are a force to be reckoned with! The Apostle Paul wrote to the church at Colossae a reminder of what we are called to be when he said in Colossians 1:27, "To them God has chosen to make known among the Gentiles the glorious riches this mystery, which is Christ in you, the hope of glory."

The extreme lows came as I perused this powerful book and realized that we have wandered so far from understanding the Kingdom of God. Our lack of understanding has allowed the devil to make fodder of God's people. We are living at a time in history where the church must not be silent. The church must rise or we are doomed. Voices of truth must declare the day of the Lord is at hand. The compass of a nation is the church of Jesus Christ and God's vessels of power! Nevertheless, the compass is destroyed when removing the drawing power of the cross, and the revelation of Christ in our lives demagnetizes it! We must rise to the occasion and recognize God has empowered you and me to make His glory known. The confused look on the face of a nation can be understood in the reflection in its eyes as it now looks upon a land that has removed truth.

Dare we be so bold to believe that Jesus has empowered us to do the work of the Kingdom? This book will empower you to walk in a new understanding of what Jesus promised in John 14:12, "Very truly I tell you, whoever believes in me will do the works I have been doing, and they will do even greater things than these, because I am going to the Father." Dare we believe that we have only begun to see the revelation of the Kingdom of God? This book will prove to you that as you lose yourself you will be empowered to greater works.

What a timeless treasure you now hold in your hands! This book is going to add to you like very few will. How? By fulfilling a promise given to us by Jesus in Matthew 6:33, "But seek first the Kingdom of God and His righteousness, and all these things shall be added to you." Thank you Pastor David Garcia for bringing forth a message that will impact generations to come!"

Patrick Schatzline
International Evangelist & Author
Remnant Ministries International

Foreword

By Bob Armstrong

To write a foreword for Dr. David Garcia is not very complex. He is totally straight-forward; in his presence with people, in his ministry; and, in his writing. David Garcia is a true "man of his word." I hate to use the terminology, but "What you see, is what you get!"

He presents the Gospel in an unashamedly way to convict and challenge the sinner. I have witnessed his style of preaching and teaching that gets inside of the sinner and lovingly convicts them of sin.

In that same loving spirit, he has pro-actively come against the "establishment Church" to convict them of their transgression. Their transgression: the present-day Church of Jesus Christ has NOT presented the ENTIRE Gospel, especially when it comes to the teaching of the Gospel of the Kingdom to the Body of Christ.

The Gospel of the Kingdom of God has been thoroughly researched by David Garcia. Sometimes, he goes against the "grain" of numerous, researched scholars on this subject; but David is NOT afraid to tell the truth.

David Garcia has a writing style that is unparalleled. He digs deep, yet he explains it in his writings in a way that even the most common folk can understand. Under the anointing, David gives very inspired insights into the Kingdom of God.

It would greatly behoove you to pay attention to this anointed teaching within this book. Not only is the Holy

Spirit imbedded within the teaching, but the teaching is absolutely earth-shaking. The Holy Spirit has not only inspired David Garcia to write, but his writing has revealed so much.

Forget your previous way of thinking about the Kingdom of God on this earth; these keen insights just might prove your original thinking wrong!

Dr. David Garcia has "hit the nail on the head." The total understanding of the "Gospel of the Kingdom" can be obtained through this very simple explanation and anointed writing of this must-read book!

Rev. Bob Armstrong
Love-Link Ministries, Bradenton, Florida

In ministry for three decades, Rev. Armstrong has trained 51,000 pastors and leaders in 40 countries in leadership conferences. Love-Link now rescues women from ISIS and rehabilitates them in safe-houses in Kurdistan. (www.lovelinkministries.com)

The Gospel of the Kingdom

Heaven's Powerful Influence on Earth

It is sad and unfortunate that most Christians will define the Kingdom of God as Jesus dying for our sins through His shed blood, and the subsequent resurrection.

Their understanding is limited to "having our sins forgiven and as a result, going to Heaven when we die." This has generally led to an anemic church in America that is limited to speaking but no visible power of demonstration in the miraculous, with the exception of a few power ministries and churches. But if that is all to the gospel or "the good news," why then did Jesus consistently warn, "Repent, for the Kingdom of Heaven is at hand" (Matthew 4:17) and "Seek first the Kingdom of God..." (Matthew 6:33) and "sent them to preach the Kingdom of God and to heal the sick." (Luke 9:2).

Some may say that was before the resurrection and that after the resurrection the primary message of the church was the cross, the blood, and salvation from our sins. While the aforementioned is critical to being "born-again," this is only the entrance to the Kingdom of God and there is so much more. Since the Church has predominantly preached salvation, it created a Heaven-minded attitude and actually assisted in carnality within the Christians.

Why then did Paul preach the gospel of the Kingdom of God: 1 Corinthians 4:20; 6:10; Romans 14:17; say in Acts 20:25 "And indeed, now I know that you all, among whom I have gone preaching the Kingdom of God, will see my face no more." The book of Acts ends with this: "Then Paul dwelt two whole years in his own rented house, and received all who came to him, preaching the Kingdom of God..." The concept of the Kingdom of God is the rulership and government of God over our lives now here on earth and that we must not only submit and allow King Jesus to govern us; but that we can bring rulership to the problems of others around us. Did Jesus not say, "...Your Kingdom come, Your will be done on earth as it is in Heaven...." The gospel is bringing the attributes of Heaven here on earth now.

Thank God that the "gospel of Christ is the power of God to salvation for everyone who believes" (Romans 1:16), but this is only the entrance into the Kingdom of God (John 3:3). Once we are saved, we realize that we are called to bring God's power and rulership to the earth by not only preaching the cross and the resurrection, but by a gospel of demonstration with signs and wonders that sinners may experience the Kingdom of God (1 Corinthians 2:1-5; 4:20). The message of the Kingdom of God is the real full-gospel, much more than speaking in tongues and moving in the gifts of the Spirit.

It is a vital message that has been sporadically preached, but generally not learned and applied by most of the Church in America and the West. This, I believe, explains why the Church in America has become very similar to the lukewarm Laodecian church, with very little power demonstration to the unsaved and compromising, unholy living. Lastly, I believe Jesus gave us a hint when He said when the end would come: "And this gospel of the Kingdom will be preached in all the world as a witness to all nations, and then the end will come." (Matthew 24:14). I believe we are living in the time when the truth of the Gospel of the Kingdom is being fully restored to the church (2 Peter 1:12) and that we will see a last day world revival and harvest highlighted by an unprecedented demonstration by God's people in healings, miracles, and signs and wonders.

It is with this anticipation and a desire to prepare and inspire the body of Christ, that this book is written.

David A. Garcia
Servant of Jesus

CHAPTER ONE

The Full Gospel Is The Kingdom Of God

This book might rattle your cage of faith. This book is about the Kingdom of God. When Jesus Christ came He didn't immediately say, "Repent! I've come to the world to die for your sins!" He said, "Repent for the Kingdom of God is at hand!" A lot of our mindsets need to be acclimated the right way.

Let's read about one-half dozen fundamental scriptures that we really need to study about the Kingdom of God:

"From that time Jesus began to preach and to say, 'Repent, for the Kingdom of Heaven is at hand.'" **Matthew 4:17**

"And as you go, preach, saying, 'The Kingdom of Heaven is at hand.'" **Matthew 10:7**

"But if I cast out demons by the Spirit of God, surely the Kingdom of God has come upon you." **Matthew 12:28**

"And this gospel of the Kingdom will be preached in all the world as a witness to all the nations, and then the end will come." **Matthew 24:14**

But He said to them, "I must preach the Kingdom of God to the other cities also, because for this purpose I have been sent." And He was preaching in the synagogues of Galilee. **Luke 4:43-44**

"But seek the Kingdom of God, and all these things

shall be added to you. Do not fear, little flock, for it is your Father's good pleasure to give you the Kingdom." **Luke 12:31-32**

To greatly assist me in my research on the Kingdom of God, I want to thank God for three men of God and for their invaluable books. If you get them, you will understand a whole lot more.

Guillermo Maldonado from Miami wrote a phenomenal book called *The Kingdom of Power*.[1] The late Myles Munroe, from the Bahamas, wrote *Rediscovering the Kingdom*.[2] Also, from the great Bethel Church in California, Bill Johnson authored *When Heaven Invades Earth*.[3] I quote them a lot in this book. I've used them to study and intertwined quotes from these three sources with a lot of things that I want to say.

Hear me! The Church has only been preaching a partial gospel; the full gospel is the Kingdom of God. I know I may offend some brethren, even among some of my preacher friends. One more time: The Church has only been preaching a partial gospel; the full gospel is the Kingdom of God!

We Pentecostal and Charismatic churches pride ourselves by saying, "You know we're a full gospel church. We believe in the baptism of the Holy Spirit and the gifts of the Spirit." That's just a part of the picture. The missing ingredient is that the Church as a whole has not been preaching the message of the Kingdom of God.

Remember: The Christ and the Kingdom of God. I believe you can't enter the Kingdom of God unless you repent and claim justification through the sacrifice of the shed blood of Jesus on the cross.

His Predecessor

Predecessor means the person that comes before you. Who came before Jesus preaching with power? John the Baptist. Read what he said.

"In those days John the Baptist came preaching in the wilderness of Judea, and saying, 'Repent for the Kingdom of Heaven is at hand!'" **Matthew 3:1-2**

His Possession

Jesus possesses and is the Kingdom. Jesus also said in **Matthew 4**, "Repent, for the Kingdom of Heaven is at hand." What did He mean?

The word Kingdom, if you have a *Strong's Exhaustive Concordance* you can reference it in #932, is *basileia*. It is a very difficult word to translate into English. We need several words to fully explain the meaning of *basileia*.

The Kingdom is Royalty

It means royalty. You know if the royal family in England came to America there would be standing ovations, there would be parades. You would have to take a course on how to curtsy and how to bow down. How much more for King Jesus?

The Kingdom is Rulership

It means rule. The Kingdom of God is the rulership of God. You can't believe in the Kingdom unless He totally takes over your life. If God's Kingdom is inside of me, that means He rules. We don't get a chance to vote. In the Kingdom of God you have no say. We do what the King says. But here is the great news; the King is a loving King! He has the very best for you! Whatever He tells you to do, the Holy Spirit will enable you to carry it out.

The Kingdom is Realm

Realm just implies the extent of the boundaries of His Kingdom. Every time someone gets saved the realm of the Kingdom of God is expanded. Every time we go to another nation, preach the Kingdom, and someone gets saved, the realm of the Kingdom of God expands.

The word sovereignty is more of the same thing. Sovereignty, in a 14 or a 15-year-old's language, means that God does what He wants, when He wants, and how He wants, without checking with anybody. God is sovereign and so when we look at His word we say, "Well, I don't agree with that!" You don't have to agree with it. You just have to do it.

The Kingdom is Royal Power

Royal power implies, in *basileia*, this Kingdom is not supposed to be stationary. You have been given the right to take what the King gives and give it to other people. That's what royal power means. Why do you need power? You need power to change people's lives and we can do that.

The King is Jesus, the constitution is the Word of God, and the citizens are those who have submitted to Him and are growing in their submission. In the Kingdom of God it's not enough to say, "Well, I became a Christian 22 years ago and I don't need to read my Bible." No, no, no! The citizens of this Kingdom not only submit to Him, but they are growing in their relationship with Him. By the way, if they comply with the King with an attitude; simply do what they are told but with a bad attitude, then they are in compliance; but they are not in submission. The King can't bless you when you are in compliance. The King can only bless you when you have a good attitude. When you say, "You know what? I don't understand everything but that is what my authority says. Bless God. Let's do it." This is what it means in Isaiah 1:19, "If you are willing and obedient you shall eat the good of the land." It is possible to be obedient (in compliance) but in your heart be unwilling (not in submission).

The Kingdom is Rulership

The Kingdom of God is the rulership of God in our lives and through our lives to the people around us. It means when I go to the restaurant after the service I take the King with me. So I act kingly, my emotions are under the King. There are no such thing as dominating moods – I'm in a bad mood, so don't mess with me – no, no, no. The King's people subjugate their moods. The King's people don't give into emotions. Whether you're going through andropause (men) or menopause (ladies) and all the other pauses, you don't take it out on people around you because the King's people have their feelings under control.

If we are the King's people, we have rulership in our lives and through our lives and bless the people around us. The King's people can bless others because they have put the devil to flight.

Therefore submit to God. Resist the devil and he will flee from you. **James 4:7**

This is a Kingdom that can't be kept inside of us. This King says, "What you have from Me, you've got to take to other people or it's not a Kingdom."

19

The Kingdom of God is the Christian taking the power of Jesus to heal and deliver others. You say, "Well, I'm not an evangelist."

Let me correct something, in the Kingdom of God we are all evangelists. In the Kingdom of God, we are all pastoral. In the Kingdom of God, we are all prophetic. In the Kingdom of God, we are all apostolic. Look at **Acts 8:4-7**:

"Therefore those who were scattered went everywhere preaching the Word. Then Philip went down to the city of Samaria and preached Christ to them. And the multitudes with one accord heeded the things spoken by Philip, hearing and seeing the miracles which he did. For unclean spirits, crying out with a loud voice, came out of many who were possessed; and many who were paralyzed and lame were healed."

That's what we should be seeing! I read the Apostle Paul in **Romans 15:18-19**, "For I will not dare to speak of any of those things which Christ has not accomplished through me, in word and deed, to make the Gentiles obedient - in mighty signs and wonders, by the power of the Spirit of God, so that from Jerusalem and round about to Illyricum I have fully preached the Gospel of Christ."

In the Kingdom of God, God is no respecter of persons. Whoever is willing to take this power out there to the grocery store, out there to the workplace, can do it. You can lay hands on people and the sick shall recover.

Please know the words of Jesus. These are not my words, but the words of Jesus.

"From that time Jesus began to preach and to say,

'Repent, for the Kingdom of Heaven is at hand.'"
Matthew 4:17

"And Jesus went about Galilee, teaching in their synagogues, preaching the gospel of the Kingdom, and healing all kinds of sickness and all kinds of disease among the people." **Matthew 4:23**

"But seek first the Kingdom of God and His righteousness, and all these things shall be added to you." **Matthew 6:33**

The Kingdom is not just about going to Heaven and being issued a harp where we play songs and sing "Kumbaya" for eternity. The Kingdom of God is Heaven invading the earth now! He says in Matthew 6:33, if you seek first the Kingdom all these things, what things? Food, clothing, and shelter will be added to you. By definition, any Christian who understands the Kingdom should never be broke, should never be homeless (of course we love people who are broke and homeless), but they should never be without food, clothing, or shelter because the King has promised it. But it is only the people who appropriate that which move into the Kingdom.

"Then Jesus went about all the cities and villages, teaching in their synagogues, preaching the gospel of the Kingdom, and healing every sickness and every disease among the people." **Matthew 9:35**

"Then Jesus said to His disciples, 'Assuredly, I say to you that it is hard for a rich man to enter the Kingdom of Heaven. And again I say to you, it is easier for a camel to go through the eye of a needle than for a rich man to enter the Kingdom of God.'" **Matthew 19:23-24**

"But I say to you, I will not drink of this fruit of the vine now on until the day when I drink it new with you in My Father's Kingdom." **Matthew 26:29**

You ask, "What do you mean by Kingdom?"

There's two terms: Kingdom of Heaven and Kingdom of God.

Many times they're used interchangeably.

Kingdom of Heaven - this is a spiritual location called Heaven from which God rules and influences the earth and the entire universe. This is God's dwelling place where His throne, court of angels, elders are found, for example, in **Revelation 4:9-10**. The Kingdom of Heaven is invisible, but when it impacts the visible world we live in, it's referred to and called the Kingdom of God.

God revealed to me the meaning because people are Heavenly minded. Everybody wants to go to Heaven, but nobody wants to die. We're so Heavenly minded we think all of our victory is in the afterlife. No, God is saying that when the Kingdom of Heaven invades the earth, your victory is now and you access it by faith.

The Kingdom of God is the actual rule of God on earth. By who? By the believers, as the Church, to continue to expand His reign through our authority in King Jesus and the power of the Holy Spirit.

Guillermo Maldonado says, "The Kingdom of God is His will and dominion exercised on earth as it is in Heaven."[4] I remember praying when I was a Catholic, "Our Father who art in Heaven, hallowed be Thy name. Thy Kingdom come, Thy will be done." When we used to say, "Thy Kingdom come," we used to think in the future when I get to Heaven. No, no, no! He's saying, "Thy Kingdom come now on the earth as it is in Heaven." Is there any hunger in Heaven? No. Is there any sickness in Heaven? No. Neither should there be here when you're walking with the King and the anointing and power of the Holy Spirit right here on earth!

Is there any lack in Heaven? No. There shouldn't be any lack in our lives. But if you're not walking with a Kingdom mentality then there will be lack.

The Kingdom of God encompasses the follow-ing: it encompasses the most important thing, salvation through the shed blood of Jesus (see **Ephesians 1:7**), and faith in the grace of God, **Ephesians 2:8-9** "For by grace have you been saved through faith, and that not of yourselves; it is the gift of God, not of works, lest anyone should boast." It encompasses the born-again experience.

John 3:3 reads, "Jesus answered and said to him, 'Most assuredly, I say to you, unless one is born again, he cannot see the Kingdom." In verse seven He says, "Do not marvel that I said to you, 'You must be born again.'" Jesus didn't go around preaching, "Be born again." This was an answer to a question of a priest named Nicodemus. He only said "born again" once.

The Word of God in **1 Peter 1:23** and Titus 3:5, says we've been regenerated, we've been born again. We need to be born again. But that was not the essence of His message.

His message was repent and go into the Kingdom of God. Thank God that the Kingdom of God encompasses sanctification or holiness and in the Kingdom of God we have a task - that you are to put off the old nature and put on the new nature.

Ephesians 4:22-24 says that. That you, not God, you put off your old nature, with the help of the Holy Spirit, "the old man which grows corrupt according to the deceitful lusts, and be renewed in the spirit [or in the attitude] of your mind, and that you put on the new man which was created according to God, in true righteousness and holiness." Kingdom people like to have good attitudes.

I've seen a lot of people – are they saved? Yes. Do they act saved? No. Do you want to be with them? No. Why? They are so negative and they are so nasty because they are not living in their Kingdom potential. You are not under the circumstance; you are above the circumstance. People say, "Well I woke up on the wrong side of the bed." Well, you shouldn't have gone to bed on the wrong side of bed. Kingdom people don't take it out on us just because they have a backache.

It includes the armor of God. **Ephesians 6:11** says to "Put on the whole armor of God." Again, in the Kingdom of God you put on the armor. I'm not going to put it on for you. In the Kingdom of God, you put on the armor. It talks about spiritual warfare. It encompasses, thank God, the message of the cross. If it wasn't for the cross, we wouldn't have the Kingdom of God. If it wasn't for the cross, we can't get into the Kingdom of God. For the cross and the death and the resurrection of Jesus are absolutely paramount to the Kingdom of God, but these things are not the only message.

The resurrection is a part of the Kingdom of God; all of the major evangelical doctrines are part of the Kingdom of God. The main message Jesus preached was the Kingdom of God. Make no mistake about it.

Jesus brought Heaven down to earth (Kingdom of Heaven). **Matthew 4:17** "From that time Jesus began to preach and to say, 'Repent, for the Kingdom of Heaven is at hand.'" What did he mean by that? He brought the realm of Heaven – meaning the Kingdom of Heaven

– into the rulership on earth. Now it's referred to as the Kingdom of God. He brought the place of Heaven, Kingdom of Heaven, to the earth with power and it becomes the Kingdom of God.

The Kingdom of Heaven is up there in the Heavenlies, in the sweet by and by. But when it comes here in a visitation of healing, when it comes here under the anointing like the anointed worship that we have, it becomes the Kingdom of God. We have to stop being so future minded that we become no earthly good. We have to be now minded; now's the time for healing, now's the time to cast out demons and God has given each of us through the power of the Holy Spirit the ability to do it.

You may ask, "Pastor, are you saying that it's my job to bring the Kingdom of God to everybody?" YES! YES! He brought the invisible Kingdom of Heaven into visible manifestations of power on earth like healing the sick and casting out demons. He said, "But if I cast out demons with the finger of God, surely the Kingdom of God has come upon you." Why is casting out demons a proof of the Kingdom of God? The Kingdom of Satan that had that person bound up for years didn't last two minutes in the presence of a daughter or son who has the power of the Kingdom of God.

Jesus is the Creator

What is God's purpose on earth? First of all, Jesus is the Creator.

Colossians 1:16 "For by Him all things were created that are in Heaven and that are on Earth, visible and invisible, whether thrones or dominions or principalities or powers. All things were created through Him and for

Him." If He's the Creator, He knows how to fix it. If He's the Creator, He knows how to kick the devil out! If He's the Creator, He knows what you are and who you are. He knew your DNA before the world began. He knows how to direct you into having real Kingdom fulfillment here on planet earth. He's not only the Creator, He's the Revealer.

Jesus is the Revealer

He reveals the Father in **John 14:8-9** "Philip said to Him, 'Lord, show us the Father, and it is sufficient for us.' Jesus said to him, 'Have I been with you so long, and yet you have not known Me, Philip? He who has seen Me has seen the Father; so how can you say, "Show us the Father'?" He wasn't the Father, but He is the exact image of the Father. The Godhead is Father, Son, and Holy Spirit. It's a mystery. Creator, Revealer, and He's Redeemer. I thank God we serve Him who is the Redeemer.

Jesus is the Redeemer

Redeem means to buy back by paying a price. Jesus paid the price. We were on the auction block of sin, on our way to hell and the Redeemer, King Jesus took our place, died for that sin, resurrected on the third day and conquered sin and death and we can have eternal life.

1 Peter 1:18-19 reads, "Knowing that you were not redeemed with corruptible things, like silver or gold, from your aimless conduct received by the tradition of your fathers, but with the precious blood of Christ, as of a lamb without blemish and without spot." Let me declare to you Jesus redeemed us from curses as well; He redeemed us from the curse of the Law.

Galatians 3:13 says, "Christ has redeemed us from the curse of the law, having become a curse for us (for it is written, "Cursed is everyone who hangs on a tree")." Kingdom people regularly break curses. I mean that is in your nature just like you eat breakfast: go ahead and break curses over somebody.

Jesus is the Destroyer

He's not only Creator, Revealer, and Redeemer, He's the Destroyer. He destroyed the works of Satan.

"For this purpose the Son of God was manifested, that He might destroy the works of the devil." I'm talking about all the works of the devil were destroyed. **1 John 3:8b**

"Having disarmed principalities and powers, He made a public spectacle of them, triumphing over them in it." **Colossian 2:15** You have a lot of intercessors now saying, "We have to come against the principalities over Europe."

If Jesus disarmed them, then why do Christians still live in defeat? Jesus gave us the initial victory over Satan, but now the Christian must apply that victory through submission to God and resistance to the devil. **James 4:7**

Jesus is the Ruler

He's the ruler of the world. Through whom? Through you and me and through the Church.

Ephesians 1:18-23 in the New Living Translation says: "I pray that your hearts will be flooded with light so that you can understand the confident hope He has given to those He called - His holy people who are

His rich and glorious inheritance." We ought to have glorious hope. "I also pray that you will understand the incredible greatness of God's power for us who believe in Him. This is the same mighty power that raised Christ from the dead and seated Him in the place of honor at God's right hand in the Heavenly realms. Now He is far above any ruler or authority or power or leader or anything else - not only in this world but also in the world to come. God has put all things under the authority of Christ and has made Him to be head over all things for the benefit of the church. And the church is His body. It is made full and complete by Christ who fills all things everywhere with Himself."

We have the authority to take it to the Kingdom of darkness. Didn't Jesus say the gates of hell shall not prevail against the Church? That's not a defensive verse; that's an offensive verse. Hell can't stop us! In The Message version it says this, "That's why, when I heard of the solid trust you have in the Master Jesus and your outpouring of love to all the followers of Jesus, I couldn't stop thanking God for you – every time I prayed, I'd think of you and give thanks. But I do more than thank. I ask the God of our Master, Jesus Christ, the God of glory – to make you intelligent and discerning in knowing him personally, your eyes focused and clear, so that you can see exactly what it is He is calling you to do. Grasp the immensity of this glorious way of life he has for his followers, oh, the utter extravagance of his work in us who trust him – endless energy, boundless strength! All this energy issues from Christ: God raised him from death and set him on a throne in deep Heaven, in charge of running the universe" **Ephesians 1:18-21** (MSG)

He rules over everything "from galaxies to governments; no name and no power is exempt from

His rule." This is forever. "He is in charge of it all. He has the final word on everything. At the center of all this, Christ rules the Church. The Church is not peripheral to the world; or not next to the world, inferior to it, but the world is peripheral to the Church." We are the head, not the tail. "The church is Christ's body, in which He speaks and acts, by which he fills everything with His presence." **Ephesians 1:22-23** (MSG)

God's going to speak to your neighbor through you. God's going to talk to the waitress at the restaurant through you. When we're praying for something, "Oh God, would you reveal Yourself?" God in His mercy does that, but He wants to speak to them directly through you. He wants to prophesy to them through you.

His Prayer

Matthew 6:10, remember "Our Father who art in Heaven, hallowed be Thy name, Thy Kingdom come, Thy will be done on earth as it is in Heaven." I just thought this was a quick prayer that we prayed. I used to pray like an auctioneer. They never understood the power of prayer through Jesus Christ and the Holy Spirit. Do you know how many supposed Christians there are that still don't understand it when He says, "Your Kingdom come now, Your will be done *now,* on the earth *now* as it is in Heaven."

Bill Johnson says, "Jesus' model reveals the two real priorities of prayer: First, intimacy with God that is expressed in worship—holy is Your name. And second, to bring His Kingdom to Earth, establishing His dominion over the needs of mankind—Your Kingdom come!"[5] If someone falls and hurts his leg, we have an opportunity to lay hands on him, and get him healed in the name of

Jesus. The anointing will increase as your knowledge of the Kingdom increases.

Myles Munroe offered, "We are praying that whatever happens in Heaven will be manifested in the earth regions."[6]

Guillermo Maldonado gives this insight, "The Lord's prayer deals with worshipping God the Father, having communion with Him, and bringing His Kingdom to earth."[7] Again, many Christians believe that the main purpose of the Kingdom is to take them to Heaven. Instead, it is clear that the purpose of the Kingdom is to bring Heaven to the earth! We must understand that our King's will, dominion, and Lordship must be carried out on the earth here and now, the same way they are carried out in Heaven."

Hallelujah! You may say, "Well, Pastor, that's not for me!" Rather stop and think, *Jesus is speaking these words to me. I must not allow my words to talk me out of the benefits of the Kingdom.* Your words have power and some of us are hung by the tongue and we disqualify ourselves, not from Heaven, but from the Kingdom of God. God can't use you if you don't believe this. God can't use you if you speak negative and eliminate yourself.

His Power

Don't you know that you have power...His power!

Matthew 4:23 tells us, "And Jesus went about all Galilee, teaching in their synagogues, preaching the gospel of the Kingdom, and healing all kinds of sickness and all kinds of disease among the people."

Luke 5:17 says, "Now it happened on a certain day, as He was teaching, that there were Pharisees and teachers of the law sitting by, who had come out of every town of Galilee, Judea, and Jerusalem. And the power of the Lord was present to heal them."

Kingdom power manifests where the Kingdom of God is expected and welcomed. The presence of God should regularly follow us. The presence of God is not just like, "Well, let's call Pastor so and so and the worship team. Let's pop in a CD so that the glory will come in the car." The glory is already with you in the car. You take the glory and the power with you. **2 Corinthians 3:18**

Jesus proclaimed the Kingdom of God, not only with words, but in demonstration of power over sickness, demons, disease, and poverty. There are many Christians who would not know what to do if a demon were to manifest in front of them. They would have to call the pastor or somebody who's anointed in deliverance ministry. You have a deliverance ministry! **Luke 4:18** All the demons are subject to you. **Luke 10:19** You don't need to call me to your house. You need to take that finger and say, "In the name of Jesus – out right now! Get out of my son! Get out of my daughter!" **Luke 11:20**

Jesus also communicated and demonstrated power in the present, in the now. He wasn't talking about the sweet by and by; He was talking about now.

The Church is called not only to communicate the Kingdom in words but in demonstration of power over demons, disease, and poverty.

Look at Paul in **1 Corinthians 2:1-5** And I, brethren, when I came to you, did not come with excellence of speech or of wisdom declaring to you the testimony of God. For I determined not to know anything among you except Jesus Christ and Him crucified. I was with you in weakness, in fear, and in much trembling. And my speech and my preaching were not with persuasive words of human wisdom, but in demonstration of the Spirit and of power, that your faith should not be in the wisdom of men but in the power of God."

That's where your faith should be! The church has a lot of speakers but very few doers; their ministry is almost exclusively speaking, but little or no demon-stration! Churches are filled where everybody faces the speaker, because he speaks, and we hear his words and then we decide if we want to listen to him or not. But our faith should not be in the wisdom of men but in the power of God. **1 Corinthians 2:5** "For the Kingdom of God is not in word but in power." **1 Corinthians 4:20**

I want to see a church of **1 Thessalonians 1:5** "For our gospel did not come to you in word only, but also in power."

The world says, "Talk is cheap." It is! Let's show them something. Let the single girl come out and show them something. Let the 14-year-old kid in middle school show them something. Let's astound the teachers in the middle school and the high school. Let's astound the Muslims with power and miracles.

His Priority

What's His priority? To give us the Kingdom. You say, "Pastor, I don't know if I can do that."

Luke 12:32 reads, "Do not fear, little flock, for it is your Father's good pleasure to give you the Kingdom," along with His power. He sealed it in His blood, guaranteed it with His resurrection. If we would seek first and above all things the Kingdom of God and His righteousness (seeking only to remain in right standing with Him) then all our needs will be provided for.

We need to preach the gospel of the Kingdom and not just the cross. The cross is the entrance to the Kingdom. Gospel means *euangelion* – the good news. Myles Munroe said, "The good news that Jesus preached (and that we should preach) is that the Kingdom of God has come to earth and, through Jesus, we can all become a part of it."[8]

This includes being born again by the blood and grace of Jesus, holiness, deliverance from demonic control, the abundant life. **John 10:10b** says, "I have come that they may have life," *zoë*, life in the maximum, spiritual and physical prosperity. **3 John 2** is not just a wish. He says, "Beloved, I pray that you may prosper in all things and be in health, just as your soul prospers." Kingdom people prosper.

Jesus will return when the gospel of the Kingdom is preached to every nation and not before then. **Matthew 24:14**

God's got a huge problem. His problem is the Church. Many Kingdom teachers agree, you cannot serve the Kingdom of God with a democratic mindset. In the Kingdom we have no choice. The King speaks, the King has written His word and when He speaks and He has written His word, we are to execute what this constitution says. It's not a question of debate or whether I agree with you or I disagree with you; the King has spoken. If you don't obey Him then He's not the King. I see Jesus as King or nothing!

I am concerned that a vast number of people in the Church of the United States and Western Europe are not really born again. Do you know why? They are in control of their lives. You cannot be born again and retain control of your life. Jesus' problem is that the Church can be divided into three basic categories:

1. FALSE CHURCH.

This includes the non-evangelical churches, the ones that don't preach the necessity of being born again, promoting humanism, and relativism, preaching a compromised historical Jesus in which works and religious acts can earn one entrance to Heaven. These are the churches that don't believe that Jonah was swallowed by a fish, or that Adam and Eve bit the fruit, that are ordaining homosexuals and condoning sin and compromise. By the way, I love homosexuals; I just want to see them in the Kingdom and until they repent, they are not going to go into the Kingdom. (**1 Corinthians 6:9-10**)

2. THE LIMITED CHURCH.

These are Evangelical and to some extent Charismatic, Pentecostal, Assemblies of God, Church of God churches who believe the following: The purpose of preaching is to win the lost and make disciples, but have limited power or limited demonstration of the power of God. However, the purpose of the church is to get those disciples into the fullness of the Kingdom. The limited church believes that the good news is only that Jesus died for the salvation of man's sins. I am saying that salvation will only qualify you to enter the doorway of the Kingdom.

Myles Munroe puts it this way, "Our problem is that we spend so much time telling people how to get into the Kingdom (by being born again) that we rarely teach them what to do once they get inside."[9] The Church has entered the door of salvation but has for the most part been stuck at the door and/or the hallway and fails to progress into the rest of the house/Kingdom in order to appropriate the abundant life of righteousness, joy, peace, prosperity and fulfillment of the maximized life.

That's why we need so much counseling! We are counseling people in their rebellion! Imagine, we are coming into the Kingdom of God. There's the door to the Kingdom – we preach, "Here's a tract. You need Jesus. Jesus loves you." There are a lot of people waiting to get in, but everybody's in the doorway. Thousands are at the doorway, but we have no power! That's like you serving me dinner or pizza in the hallway right outside your door and you never invite me in to the dining room. King Jesus doesn't want to only be in the hallway. He wants to go into the dining room. Myles Munroe claims, "So much of the time today we get the message wrong by preaching the good news of Heaven. The two are not the same. We tell people to put their faith in Jesus for salvation and in turn we focus on Heaven as our goal and destination."[10] People struggling with the problems of life on Earth need a message to help them now. The rulership of God has come to Earth and we can all experience abundant life now!

3. THE REMNANT CHURCH.

I want to be a part of the remnant church. This is the Church that's preaching the whole gospel of the Kingdom of God. If you don't have the mindset of the Kingdom, you can't have the results of the Kingdom. What are the results of the Kingdom? The dead raised, cancer cancelled, people getting saved, prophecy and the gifts of the Holy Spirit flowing out of your life; but you've got to have a Kingdom mindset.

Acts 1:3 "To whom He also presented Himself alive after His suffering by many infallible proofs, being seen by them during forty days and speaking of the things pertaining to the Kingdom of God."

Acts 8:12 "But when they believed Philip as he preached the things concerning the Kingdom of God and the name of Jesus Christ, both men and women were baptized."

Acts 14:22 "Strengthening the souls of the disciples, exhorting them to continue in the faith, and saying, "We must through many tribulations enter the Kingdom of God."' And then the church wonders why we suffer.

Acts 19:8 "And he went into the synagogue and spoke boldly for three months, reasoning and persuading concerning the things of the Kingdom of God."

Acts 20:25 "And indeed, now I know that you all, among whom I have gone preaching the Kingdom of God, will see my face no more."

Acts 28:23 "So when they had appointed him a day [this is Paul], many came to him at this lodging, to whom he explained and solemnly testified of the Kingdom of God, persuading them concerning Jesus from both the law of Moses and the Prophets, from morning till evening."

Acts 28:31 "[Paul] preaching the Kingdom of God and teaching the things which concern the Lord Jesus Christ with all confidence, no one forbidding him."

Jesus again said in **Matthew 24:14** "And this gospel of the Kingdom will be preached in all the world as a witness to all the nations, and then the end will come."

One moment with the King is worth a lifetime of labor without Him. I want to pray for an anointing of the King upon your life.

Father, in Jesus' name, I declare the Kingdom of God on you. I speak and decree and prophesy Heaven's place in your life right now. I declare that you are a new creation. I declare that you will no longer limit God. I declare Kingdom victory over the wiles of the flesh. Kingdom victory over all carnality, works of the flesh. Kingdom victory over all of the demonic. You will not need a deliverance ministry; you will be the deliverance ministry in the name of Jesus. I declare prophetic intercession over you. I declare that as you wait upon God the oracles of God and the revelations of God will flow out of your mouth and you will only pray that which God wants you to pray. I declare and decree right now, in the name of Jesus, the gifts of the Holy Spirit flowing in and through you changing people's lives around you. I declare that you are a minister of God. I declare right now that you have wisdom, sanctification, and redemption all wrapped into one because of the Kingdom of God. I speak that to you right now in Jesus' name. Hallelujah!

CHAPTER TWO

Heaven's Powerful Influence On People Here On Earth

"And I also say to you that you are Peter, and on this rock I will build My church, and the gates of Hades shall not prevail against it. And I will give you the keys of the Kingdom of Heaven, and whatever you bind on earth will be bound in Heaven, and whatever you loose on earth will be loosed in Heaven."
Matthew 16:18-19

"But seek the Kingdom of God, and all these things shall be added to you. Do not fear, little flock, for it is your Father's good pleasure to give you the Kingdom."
Luke 12:31-32

"Now when He was asked by the Pharisees when the Kingdom of God would come, He answered them and said, "The Kingdom of God does not come with observation; nor will they say, 'See here!' or 'See there!' For indeed, the Kingdom of God is within you."
Luke 17:20-21

Key Take Away: The Kingdom of God is Heaven's powerful influence on people here on earth by Christians moving in the power of the Holy Spirit.

The Kingdom of God works when you are available to be a conduit to touch people with that power.

A Kingdom has contents. Like any Kingdom, the Kingdom of God contains ten features. You just think of a Kingdom that you know on earth.

1. First of all, a Kingdom has a King and a Lord –

Jesus Christ. All authority flows from Him and His word is supreme. Nothing that is of leadership or power or authority happens without the King.

2. **A Kingdom has a territory.** That territory is the domain over which the king exercises authority is planet earth. **Psalm 24:1** "The earth is the Lord's, and all its fullness, the world and those who dwell therein." You'll look around and say, "Well, I don't see the Lord ruling the earth." He rules through His Church.

3. **A Kingdom needs a constitution.** The constitution of the Kingdom is the Word of God. It's the Bible. God's Word is our constitution. That tells you what to do and what not to do.

4. **A Kingdom needs citizens.** We need a citizenry. Myles Munroe writes, "A citizenry is the people that live under the rule of the King. Citizenship in a Kingdom is not a right, but a privilege...the benefits and privileges of a Kingdom are only accessible to citizens and therefore, the favor of the king is always a privilege."[11] Favor means divine, preferential treatment. Favor means "to highly esteem."

"The favor of the king is always a privilege. Once one becomes a citizen of the Kingdom, all the rights of citizenship are at the citizen's pleasure. The king is obligated to care and protect all of His citizens and their welfare is a reflection on the king himself." What do people think of Jesus when they look at you? "The number one goal of a citizen in a Kingdom is to submit to the king."[12] Submit does not mean merely to comply. Submit means you say, "Yes Sir." There's no voting.

There's nothing like that. "Seeking only to remain in right standing with Him. This is called righteousness."[13] Righteousness means that you are standing right with the King. This is why the priority of all men is to seek His Kingdom.

Matthew 6:33 tells us, "But seek first the Kingdom of God and His righteousness [and right standing with Him], and all these things shall be added to you."

5. **A Kingdom needs the law.** The law institutes the standards and principles established by the king himself. From John Bevere's book and teachings, *Undercover,* "In our culture it is hard to understand Kingdom principles because we tend to view everything with a democratic mindset."[14] What does that mean? That means there is no voting in the Kingdom. We don't have a democracy; we have a theocracy. You don't get to pick and choose what you want to obey Jesus on. You do what He says. If you don't do it, it's called rebellion. The law institutes the standards and principles established by the king himself, by which his Kingdom will function and be administered. A code of ethics is the acceptable conduct of the citizens in the Kingdom and their representatives of the Kingdom. We represent the King of Kings. Let's look like representatives; let's act like we're representatives. Let's act like we're ambassadors. I'm not saying you need to come to church with a three-piece suit and a tie but, you know what, let's do your best to represent the King. We need to look like an ambassador of the King and we need to speak like one. Always be conscious of that.

6. **A Kingdom needs an army.** The angels of God are the military component of the Kingdom in the Heavenlies, in the sky, in space. The Church is the military component of the Kingdom on earth and on earth we have angelic help. The Church is to engage in spiritual warfare. We've been given the keys to the Kingdom.

Matthew 16:18-19 And I also say to you that you are Peter, and on this rock I will build My church, and the gates of Hades shall not prevail against it. And I will give you the keys of the Kingdom of Heaven, and whatever you bind on earth will be bound in Heaven, and whatever you loose on earth will be loosed in Heaven.

Whatever we loose on earth shall be loosed in Heaven. God will build His Church and the gates of hell don't prevail against us. Gates don't attack. We attack the gates of hell.

2 Timothy 2:3-4 "You therefore must endure hardship as a good soldier of Jesus Christ. No one engaged in warfare entangles himself with the affairs of this life, that he may please Him who enlisted him as a soldier [or who drafted him as a soldier]."

You are a soldier! You may say, "Well, I don't remember joining up!" You joined up when you repented of your sins and asked Jesus to be your Lord and Savior. That is when you immediately signed up. **2 Timothy 2:4** "No one engaged in warfare entangles himself with the affairs of this life, that he may please him who enlisted Him as a soldier." "Well how long is this service?" Until He comes and even then in Heaven we'll be serving Him.

The battlefield is the mind!

2 Corinthians 10:3-6 For though we walk in the flesh, we do not war according to the flesh. For the weapons of our warfare **are** not carnal but mighty in God for pulling down strongholds, casting down arguments and every high thing that exalts itself against the knowledge of God, bringing every thought into captivity to the obedience of Christ, and being ready to punish all disobedience when your obedience is fulfilled.

Ephesians 6:10-17 Finally, my brethren, be strong in the Lord and in the power of His might. Put on the whole armor of God that you may be able to stand against the wiles of the devil. For we do not wrestle against flesh and blood, but against principalities, against powers, against the rulers of the darkness of this age, against spiritual **hosts** of wickedness in the Heavenly **places**. Therefore, take up the whole armor of God, that you may be able to withstand in the evil day, and having done all, to stand. Stand therefore, having girded your waist with truth, having put on the breastplate of righteousness, and having shod your feet with the preparation of the gospel of peace; above all, taking the shield of faith with which you will be able to quench all the fiery darts of the wicked one. And take the helmet of salvation, and the sword of the Spirit, which is the word of God;

Ephesians 2:10 says that we were created to do good works. "We were created before the foundation of the world to do good works which God prepared beforehand that we should walk in them." How interesting! Good works is mowing somebody's lawn, doing them a favor to attract them to the King.

1 John 3:8 "For this purpose was the Son of God manifest that He might destroy the works of Satan."

Ephesians 2:10 says that we were created to do good works. Jesus came to destroy the works of Satan. What does the word "works" mean? Works here is the word *ergon* in the Greek and it means the business, the labor, and deeds. So the good works of the church includes destroying the business, labor, and deeds of Satan in our lives and in other people's lives.

You need to evict hell out of your life. You were created to destroy the works of Satan. You were not created to be a victim; you were created to be a victor. You were also created to bring destruction to the devil in Walmart, in your school, in your high school, in your college campus, in your job. Now use wisdom because you're not getting paid to kick the devil out. You can't tell your boss, "Hey man! I'm kicking the devil out!" You'll get fired. You need to use wisdom.

7. **The Kingdom of God is a family**. What is the key word? Relationships. Relationships in the Kingdom are critical and the Church must realize we are a close-knit family with one Father. In the Kingdom, Jesus is both King and elder brother and as a family we are to walk in love, forgiveness, and forbearance. However, you don't get to choose your family. Do you know someone who has brothers and sisters that they wish were somebody else's brothers and

sisters? In your spiritual family you don't get to pick and choose who's your family member. You don't choose their color, their personality. You don't choose where you live. We're all part of the family! The Father chose us! The Father did not consult with you and I about who's next in the Kingdom of God. When the bus of the Kingdom of God came around and picked people up, the driver, King Jesus, didn't consult you about who He should save.

Ephesians 3:14-15 "For this reason I bow my knees to the Father of our Lord Jesus Christ, from whom the whole family in Heaven and earth is named."

1 Timothy 5:1-2 "Do not rebuke an older man, but exhort him as a father, younger men as brothers, older women as mothers, younger women as sisters, with all purity." We're all brothers and sisters.

Hebrews 2:10-17 "For it was fitting for Him, for whom are all things and by whom are all things, in bringing many sons to glory, to make the captain of their salvation perfect through sufferings. For both He who sanctifies and those who are being sanctified are all of one, for which reason He is not ashamed to call them brethren, saying: 'I will declare Your name to My brethren; in the midst of the assembly I will sing praise to You.' And again: 'I will put My trust in Him.' And again: 'Here am I and the children whom God has given Me.' Inasmuch then as the children have partaken of flesh and blood, He Himself likewise shared in the same, that through death He might destroy him who had the power of death, that is, the devil, and release those who through fear of death were all their lifetime subject to bondage."

He does not give aid to angels, but He does give aid to the seed of Abraham. Therefore, in all things He had to be made like His brethren, that He might be a merciful and faithful High Priest in things pertaining to God, to make propitiation for the sins of the people.

Jesus is your older brother. He's not only King, He's the older brother.

8. **The Kingdom of God is also a commonwealth**. Did you ever wonder where that word comes from? It means that the wealth should be common. A commonwealth is the economic system of a Kingdom which guarantees each citizen equal access to financial security. It is the king's desire that all his citizens benefit from the wealth and health of the Kingdom, but it is up to each citizen to appropriate. Appropriate means that you make it happen. It's available; but you've got to possess it. You must understand this: the giving is God's; the taking is ours. We have to appropriate the benefits of the Kingdom through faith, then submission, obedience, and wisdom.

Luke 12:22-24 Then He said to His disciples, "Therefore I say to you, do not worry about your life, what you will eat; nor about the body, what you will put on. Life is more than food, and the body is more than clothing. Consider the ravens, for they neither sow nor reap, which have neither storehouse nor barn; and God feeds them. Of how much more value are you than the birds?"

If you're not doing those you can't have the benefits of the commonwealth. That's why He says in Luke 12:31-32 – "Do not fear, little flock, for it is your Father's good pleasure to give you the Kingdom."

I was talking to a sister in the church and she gave me her take on it and I loved it! She said, "Pastor, I think He calls them 'little flock' because, you know, us not so important people can also have the Kingdom like the real big important people." Grab ahold of this truth: the Kingdom is yours, but you've got to take it. You have to take it.

3 John 2 "Beloved, I pray that you may prosper in all things and be in health, just as your soul prosper."

9. **In the Kingdom of God there is honor.** Another word for honor is respect, pre-ferential treatment, esteemed highly. In the Kingdom, honor is bestowed to all: to those in authority above us, to those of equal authority, and to those under our authority.

A culture of respect and honor is to be exercised. Do you know what that means? If you are the boss, give honor to the people who work for you. Don't give them a hard time. If you are an employee, don't give your boss a hard time; you give him honor. If you got a mother and a father give them honor, no matter what.

The Characteristics Of The Kingdom Of God

The Kingdom of God is a supernatural Kingdom. It's not physically here like Washington D.C. or Times Square. No, no. It's not of this world. Jesus said in **John 18:36**, "My Kingdom is not of this world." It's not here on earth but yet it functions through us. In **Luke 17:20-21** Jesus said, "The Kingdom of God does not come with observation." You can't see it. "The Kingdom of God is within you." God is saying, "My rulership is within you."

Let's look at a couple of quotes from Guillermo Maldonado. What do you mean by a supernatural Kingdom? "It is the life of God exercising its influence on earth as the power of the Holy Spirit through our humanity."[15] People say, "Show me the Kingdom." When you and I move in the gifts and miracles and love they will see the Kingdom. He goes on to say, "The Kingdom reveals itself visibly through miracles and signs of God's unconditional love."[16] You may say, "Well Pastor, I'm not a healing evangelist." Let me explain: You don't have any less of the Kingdom of God than that evangelist does. You don't have any less of the Kingdom of God than any man greatly used of God.

"Pastor, I'm new. Who are those people?" They are people who are greatly used of God but, you know what, God wants to greatly use YOU! God's given you the keys to the Kingdom. Any of us can move in such power that we can open up the eyes of the blind, the ears of the deaf, and we can curse cancer. **John 14:12** We can do that, but we've got to understand that we have been given the authority and the will of God to do it. It's a Kingdom of power, not just words.

1 Corinthians 4:20 "For the Kingdom of God is not in word but in power." What do they call people like me? They ought to call us doers. You ought to be doing something. Don't talk about power; show me the power. "Show me the beef!" as the television commercial used to say. Show me the money! Show it to me! You will not get anyone healed in the name of Allah. You will not get anyone healed in the name of Buddha. But in the name of Jesus – the King of Kings, the one who died and rose again from the dead – the lame will walk and the sick will recover in the name of Jesus!

What do we mean by power? The Kingdom was not to be proclaimed with words only in an abstract way. When you talk to somebody about Jesus, don't use just words. Pray for an opportunity when they say, "I'm not feeling good." Let me lay hands on you and grab their hand and shake them. They'll say, "What are you doing?" Then say, "I'm bringing the Kingdom of God to you. I'm praying for you in the name of Jesus. Since you say, 'Seeing is believing,' well, you can see soon."

The Kingdom reveals itself visibly through miracles and signs of unconditional love. Nobody is going to want you to pray for them if you're nasty, if you're hard to live with, or if you're hard to work with. I wouldn't want you to pray for me and you wouldn't want me to pray for you if I'm always offending you and in an irritable mood.

It was always meant to be announced with power and in the present and in the now! The Kingdom of God is for right now. It's not for in the sweet by and by. Right now!

1 Thessalonians 1:5 "For our gospel did not come to you in word only, but also in power, and in the Holy

49

Spirit and in much assurance." You might say, "Well, you know that was Paul and Peter and them. That's not me." In the Kingdom of God, we're all filled with the power.

It is to be preached with demonstration of power. People in this world say, "Seeing is believing. I want to feel something." Why do you think the occult is so popular? Why do you think people are going to mediums and young people are running to psychics? They want some power. It's time that the Church put some power with their belief. We have the power!

1 Corinthians 2:1-5 "And I, brethren, when I came to you, did not come with excellence of speech or of wisdom declaring to you the testimony of God. For I determined not to know anything among you except Jesus Christ and Him crucified. I was with you in weakness, in fear, and in much trembling. And my speech and my preaching were not with persuasive words [not with beautiful notes with matching letters and blank spaces for you to write] of human wisdom, but in demonstration of the Spirit and of power, that your faith should not be in the wisdom of men but in the power of God."

We should have faith in God's power! It should be working in the present! It should be working right now! It's an unshakable Kingdom. I was watching a television show the other day. They were talking about storing food, doing this, all the grief, the volcanoes, etc. It would scare an atheist into the Kingdom. I sat there and went, "Wait a minute! The Bible says in **Hebrews 12:28**, 'Therefore, since we are receiving a Kingdom which cannot be shaken, let us have grace, by which we may serve God acceptably with reverence and godly fear.'"

We should not be afraid that the food is going to run

out. I'm going to have godly fear, not worldly fear, and so should you. This world is being shaken physically, politically, and economically in many ways. Jesus is coming very soon whether He comes pre, mid, or post tribulation; that's not my concern. Jesus is coming soon!

If we are under the covering and the authority of the Kingdom, we cannot be shaken ever! You can't be shaken! You can't be moved away!

Luke 6:47-48 (remember the words flood and stream represent crisis and emergencies) – "Whoever comes to Me, and hears My sayings and does them, I will show you whom he is like: He is like a man building a house, who dug deep and laid the foundation on the rock. And when the flood arose, the stream beat vehemently against that house, and could not shake it, for it was founded on the rock."

Is your life on the rock today? If it is, no crisis should shake you! Stay under the covering of the Kingdom. It's a Kingdom you can experience now! I thank God for the sweet by and by; my father is up there and many of our loved ones are up there, but I'm not looking to being up there, I am looking at right now, right here, today!

Matthew 12:28 (NLT) "But if I am casting out demons by the Spirit of God, then the Kingdom of God has arrived among you."

I regularly cast out demons by the power of God. It proves to people that the Kingdom of God is here. Demons are very obedient. Demons are more obedient than some Christians that I know. I tell a demon to leave,and it leaves because of Jesus. I tell a Christian something and he goes, "Let me pray about it. Let me think about it. I don't agree with you. I'm going to find another church. I think I'll find another pastor."

We don't have to wait to die to go to Heaven and experience it. You can have Heaven on earth right now. As an ex-Catholic, I remember praying the Lord's Prayer, "Our Father, who art in Heaven, hallowed be Thy name. Thy Kingdom come, Thy will be done on earth as it is in Heaven." "You mean I can have the Kingdom on earth?" That's the will of God.

Is there any hunger in Heaven? No, there shouldn't be here. Is there any sickness in Heaven? No, there shouldn't be here. Is there any frustration in Heaven? No, there shouldn't be here. Is there any moodiness in Heaven?

It is more than forgiveness of sins and a future Heaven. I don't know about you, but I want more. The Kingdom is the abundant life now! I talk to some Christians and you would think Jesus never came. "How are you doing?" "Oh, how much time do you have? So many things are going wrong!" I don't know about you but **John 10:10** says, "The thief [Satan] does not come except to steal, and to kill, and to destroy. I have come that they may have life [zoe – the maximized life], and that they may have it more abundantly." God wants you to have the maximized life right now! Right now!

The Character of the Kingdom

We can recognize the Kingdom in our midst when we experience, and live the following three character traits should hallmark Kingdom people. I mean people who believe in the blood of Jesus and that He went to the cross? That's just part of it. Yes, we enter the Kingdom with that, but you don't stay in the doorway.

Romans 14:17 "For the Kingdom of God is not eating and drinking, but righteousness and peace and joy in the Holy Spirit." Righteousness has three basic meanings: Righteousness means being in good standing with God by the forgiveness and redemption we receive through Christ's death and resurrection. Thank God for the blood of Jesus. But it also means submitting with a good attitude. It's submitting yourself to be accountable to God for your thoughts, words, and actions and allowing Him to correct you. He wants to correct you and guide you in the paths of righteousness.

Oh how we love **Psalm 23:3** "He restores my soul; He leads me in the paths of righteousness…" God says submitting to the King and I'm not the King, He is. Righteousness means putting on the personality of God as it says in **Micah 6:8** "What does the Lord require of you but to do justly, to love mercy, and to walk humbly with your God?" The Kingdom of God is righteousness.

The Kingdom of God is also peace. **Isaiah 9:6-7**, "For unto us a child is born, unto us a Son is given; and the government will be upon His shoulder." But before the government is on His shoulder, His government wants to rule your heart. He wants to govern you. It means He talks, you jump; He says, you do.

James 2:19 tells us you believe in God, you do good; the demons believe and they tremble. Sometimes there is not enough trembling in the house of God. There are three types of peace, first of all, peace with God. This occurs at salvation. **Romans 5:1** "Therefore, having been justified by faith, we have peace with God through our Lord Jesus Christ." Then there's the peace of God. This is direction. It says in **Philippians 4:6-7**

"Be anxious for nothing, but in everything by prayer and supplication, with thanksgiving, let your requests be made known to God; and the peace of God, which surpasses all understanding, will guard your hearts and minds through Christ Jesus."

Your spirit is right underneath your belly button. You ever want to do something and your head says, "It's good." But you get the clammiest feeling. You get this feeling, "I'd better not do that" and your head says, "What are you waiting for?" And your spirit says, "You'd better not do it." Then when you do it, you hear this, "I shouldn't have done it?" If you're married your husband or wife says, "I told you so! I told you so! I told you so!" Everything should be established in the mouth of two witnesses.

There's another peace of God. This is reconciliation. Every time you see someone get saved that is the Kingdom of God. **Colossians 1:19-20** – "For it pleased the Father that in Him all the fullness should dwell, and by Him to reconcile [that means bring together two people that were enemies] all things to Himself, by Him, whether things on earth or things in Heaven, having made peace through the blood of His cross."

Then there's joy. There's a difference between joy and happiness because **James 1:2** says, "My brethren, count it all joy when you fall into various trials." Happiness belongs in the realm of the soul, mind, emotions, and will. Joy belongs in the realm of the spirit. Big difference! Happiness is connected with what's happening outside of me. Joy is connected with who I have inside of me. No man or woman can make you happy. You decide to be happy and then he or she can add value to your happiness.

Joy is divine poise in times of trouble. Give me another word for poise – being cool; be calm, be cool. Joy is quiet confidence that no matter what is happening God's going to see me through. Hallelujah! Glory to God! If Christians had more joy, there would be more people in church.

Guillermo Maldonado says, "The Holy Spirit is the administrator and executor of the Kingdom; He is the only one who can reveal things of the Kingdom of its King."[17]

1 Corinthians 2:11 says, "For what man knows the spirit of the man which is in him? Even so no one knows the things of God except the Spirit of God." It's the Holy Spirit that speaks to you. How does the Holy Spirit sound? He sounds like your voice, just a little calmer. He'll tell you, "David, don't do that. Go say you're sorry." I don't want to say I'm sorry. "I didn't ask your opinion." You know it's the Holy Spirit because usually He tells you things you don't want to hear.

"Without the Holy Spirit there is no Kingdom or government of God,"[18] says Guillermo Maldonado. Prayer worship, and intimacy are the keys that attract the manifested presence of God on earth. That's when He shows up in an area and there's two levels of His presence. First of all, there's the anointing. That's a visitation on an individual.

Isaiah 10:27 says the anointing shall remove burdens and destroy yokes. A yoke is a bondage; a burden is a problem they are carrying. The anointing removes the burden and it destroys yokes. But the glory is a visitation over a whole area. I want to warn you about the glory. I learned this from John Bevere in his book *The Fear of the Lord*[19]—make sure you're living right when you call or sing about the glory because judgment comes after the glory. So when you say, "Oh God, give me the glory," and you are treating your wife and children unjustly, and walking in carnality, you are going to get judged. You're going to get a holy smack from Heaven. Don't ask for the glory if you are not ready for it.

The Commencement of the Kingdom of God

Commencement can also mean coming or starting. You need to be born again. **John 3:5-7** "Jesus answered, 'Most assuredly, I say to you, unless one is born of water and the Spirit, he cannot enter the Kingdom of God. That which is born of the flesh is flesh, and that which is born of the Spirit is spirit. Do not marvel that I said to you, 'You must be born again.'"

Guillermo Maldonado says, "There is no entry into the Kingdom of God except by the new birth." [20] "Whole denominations have been started by when they said, 'born of water,' and then, 'born of the Spirit.'"[18] Stop, stop, stop. Jesus was answering a question of a Jewish priest named Nicodemus. He said to Nicodemus, "You must be born again," or you must be born twice. **John 3:7** You see, Jesus means something spiritual, but all Nicodemus can think of is natural. He says, "How can a man return to his mother's womb when he's old?" What's inside the womb? There is a fluid called amniotic fluid, this is the water Jesus is referring to, the baby is in there swimming. He says how can I go back?

Number one. You must be born twice. Once naturally, that's what being "born of water" means; it refers to the amniotic fluid in your mother's womb. Then you have to be born a second time, spiritually.

That is when God enters your life. If you're born once, you'll die twice; but if you are born twice, you'll die only once. Think about that for a moment! Meaning: if you're born physically and you're never born spiritually, you're going to go to hell. But if you're born physically and spiritually, you're going to go to Heaven.

Number two. This happens with the following: one is convicted. Pastor, what does that mean? It means that you hear the Word of Godand it steps on your toes. You feel bad about the sins in your life when someone shares the Word of Godwith you personally or through preaching. Conviction is good because it's the first step to getting right. Then you repent. Repent means you turn around. You repent of your sin and you ask Jesus to be your Lord and Savior. **Acts 3:19-20** "Repent therefore and be converted, that your sins may be blotted out."

Number three. Guillermo Maldonado says that simultaneous with this born again experience "a total separation from the curse of sin must take place; the umbilical cord of iniquity that connects us to sin and the rebellious nature must be cut. The Kingdom is not a mere 'remedy' it involves becoming a new creation."[21]

2 Corinthians 5:17 "Therefore, if anyone is in Christ, he is a new creation." In the economy of the Kingdom, we must humble ourselves before we are exalted. We must give in order to receive; we must serve in order to be great; and we must die [to our self-will] in order to live. Accordingly, we must die to our own 'government.'

There used to be an old television program called "Who's the Boss?" Let me ask you something – "Who's the boss of your life?" We will either be bossed around by our selfish desires, opinions, and personal 'vote' – or we will surrender ourselves to God, so that we may truly live in Him and in the Kingdom. In the Kingdom there is no voting. You don't get to choose who's the king. By the way, there are only two kings: Jesus and you. To quote S.D. Gordon, "Every heart has a throne and a cross. If Jesus is on the throne then you are on the cross, but if self is on the throne that means Jesus is still on the cross."[22]

My question to you is, is there a crucifix in your heart? If there is, you need to get saved. You need to get born again. This is what King Jesus says to you, "You haven't contributed anything to the salvation of mankind. You say that I'm King, but then you argue with Me when I tell you I don't want you to go out with that guy, when I tell you don't marry that woman, when I tell you to drop those drugs you're taking, and stop undressing the women in the house of God with your lustful eyes."

True repentance involves a new frame of mind that reflects a change in attitude. Repentance also indicates our desire not to rule ourselves any longer but to be ruled by God, according to His government. Thus, repentance causes sin to die. Although repentance is required for entering the Kingdom, we must also constantly seek to renew our thoughts and ways in accordance with God's thoughts and ways and daily submit our lives to Him, so that we will continue to walk in the right direction.

True repentance must be whole-hearted and encompass more than a desire to escape hell. It is turning from being our own authority - choice of career, what business to start, where we want to live, who we want to marry, choice of church, choice to stay married, etc. - without consulting God. I'm amazed that when I greet guests in my church on Sunday morning, they often say, "We decided to come here because we like your children's church, the bathrooms are clean, this and that." I think to myself: *So you made a decision without even asking the King?*

Thank God for our bathrooms, thank God for our children's church, but the main question is this: "Is God calling you here?" True repentance places us from this day forward under God's authority and government, allowing Him to have the final say and rulership in our lives. True repentance means making every decision to be based on God's Word and Kingdom principle and commandments. True repentance means I now live to please the King and will not do anything without His consent, authority, and guidance. The majority of professing Christians in America, most likely, are not truly born again. They still retain control, rulership, and government over their choices. Who's really the boss when you make choices? "Nobody tells me what to do;" "I make up my own mind." Then you need the King. Maybe you're not really born again. This is why they live in defeat, they blame others, they blame the President, they blame the government, they blame Capitol Hill, they even blame God and live a life full of complaint, defeat, or mediocrity. Mediocrity means average. This is when the people in your school and in your job say, "Oh, you're a Christian? I didn't know you were a Christian." Of course not, you act just like everybody else. Their lives are usually ruled by self-interest, feelings, or works of the flesh.

You know the works of the flesh, **Galatians 5:19-21** – outbursts of wrath, anger, adultery, fornication, etc. I'm going to ask you to say this out loud with me. I call it the Pledge of Allegiance to the Lord Jesus Christ:

I pledge allegiance to King Jesus, the Creator and Lord of the Universe and to His government over my life. I pledge allegiance to His word and His blood, which seals my covenant with Him. I choose to live according to His word and the Holy Spirit's prompting. I die to my own authority, choices, desires, feelings, and from this day forward I will allow King Jesus to have the final say and rulership in my life. I will not consciously do anything without His consent, authority, or guidance. Hallelujah!

1 John 4:17 "And you will have confidence in the Day of Judgment."

CHAPTER THREE

Obedience To The Covenant

The Kingdom of God is the government of God. The Kingdom of God is the control of God in your life. I thank God for the cross. I thank God for the blood and the resurrection, but that's not the whole gospel. That's only the beginning. Jesus came preaching a gospel of the Kingdom. If you don't believe me go to an exhaustive concordance, that's a dictionary of all the Bible scriptures, and look up "Kingdom of God." You will find so many. Paul preached the Kingdom of God; Jesus preached the Kingdom of God. The Kingdom of God is the rulership of God. The Kingdom of God is Heaven coming down to earth. The Kingdom of God is when Heaven invades the earth and kicks out disease, sickness, and poverty. Everything in the Kingdom is conditional on the covenant.

"Then God blessed them, and God said to them, "Be fruitful and multiply; fill the earth and subdue it; have dominion over the fish of the sea, over the birds of the air, and over every living thing that moves on the earth." **Genesis 1:28**

"Lest Satan should take advantage of us; for we are not ignorant of his devices." **2 Corinthians 2:11**

"[God] disarmed the principalities and powers that were ranged against us **and** made a bold display **and** public example of them, in triumphing over them in Him and in it [the cross]." **Colossians 2:15 (AMP)**

"But seek first the Kingdom of God and His

righteousness, and all these things shall be added to you." **Matthew 6:33**

Key Take Away: We must recognize the kingdom concept of covenant and apply it to our daily living.

Seek first the rulership of God, seek first the ownership of God, seek first the government of God in your life and all of its righteousness and all of these things that you need: food, clothing, shelter, healing, etc. will be given to you.

The Definition of the Covenant

Let's look at the definition of the covenant. Unfortunately, in the West, we don't understand this like maybe the Native Americans or the Africans or the Easterner, but every culture had covenants. The word covenant in its most basic form means "to cut." It means to cut and draw blood. Leviticus tells us that life is in the blood. In a covenant, two people exchange their life. The phrase "to cut the covenant" signifies two people making an agreement. This particular agreement is to make a pact, a treaty sort of like a contract with each other and sealing it with the shedding of blood. Did you ever hear the terms two American Indians saying, "We are blood brothers?" That wasn't just in cowboy, western movies. Many Native Americans in the past would cut their wrists and draw blood and then they would join the two bloods together and they would say, "We are making a covenant between our families. What's yours is mine. What's mine is yours. If you're threatened, I will come to your rescue. If I'm threatened, you will come to my rescue." They meant it and there was a severe penalty if you didn't keep that.

During the Old Testament times, it was common

practice that when a covenant was established, an animal was cut in half, in two; each partner placed parallel to each other (north to south) meaning if I cut a goat in half I would put one over here and one over here. What they would do is they would walk in a figure eight in between both of them. While I was doing that I would say the blessings of this covenant are protection, health, provision and the curses of this covenant are that I would lose everything. I would sacrifice my health and when they finished that it was sealed. Blood was splattered in between them. As they were walking their sandals were filled with blood. It was sealed with blood. You knew the consequences. You can read that in **Genesis 15:9-19**. That's the definition of the covenant.

The Description of a Contemporary Covenant

Then there is the description of a contemporary covenant. If I was sixteen years old I might say, "Man, that's old stuff; what's that got to do with me? I don't do covenants today." Yes, you do! You do it if you want to get married with wedding vows. We make a covenant with God and each other. They're called vows. "On this day I take you to be my lawful wedded wife; I promise you that I will do this, that, this, that, and the other." Then we don't do it. The wife says, "I pledge to you my love forever and ever." A couple of years down the road they're not even married anymore. Why is it that we make pledges to each other? We say, "I do" and then we don't. You might say, "Well, that's just a wedding covenant, everybody expects it." My friend, we have 30 year olds that have been married and divorced three times. In **2 Timothy 3** it says in the last days there will be truce breakers. The Greek word there is "covenant breakers." We take marriage too lightly.

In real estate purchases there're a legal contract, a mortgage, stipulations for foreclosure and that comes from covenant language. If you do this, the house is yours. If you don't do it, it will go to the bank. That's why I tell a lot of people, "Are you still paying for your house?" You think you own it, just stop making the payments and you'll find out who owns it. There are contracts of professional athletes with a team. Nowadays, we have baseball agents and football agents and they make a contract for ten years and three years later, they break it because they want to be a Super Bowl champion. In America, England, and Canada we know how to break contracts and covenants.

How about vows to become an American citizen? "I pledge to defend the constitution of the United States of America." Yet over 250 Americans that took that pledge are now in the Middle East fighting for ISIS to kill Americans."[23] If I was the president, I would revoke their citizenship. I think we're much too lenient with these matters.

When we got saved, we joined the covenant that says Jesus is the King; the Christians are my family. I can't choose my family. I'm going to love them; I might not be close to all of them, but I'm going to do my best to respect and love them. If they are human enough to step on my toes, I will forgive them immediately. There is no, "I'm going to pray about it. I'm going to go see the psychiatrist first and see what she says." When you have Jesus, you have *zoë* life (life on the highest level) **John 10:10b**. You have everything you need to obey God.

Covenants are very decisive. You go in all the way. There's no going back. Let me give you an example.

I've got some ball players in my church, so I'm going to write this in sports language. There's a great player in the NFL. He was one of the finest half-backs and receivers ever to come out of college to play in the NFL. He is now on his third team in four years. He was drafted by one team; but only lasted there a year. They traded him to a top contender team in the NFL where he lasted there a year and a half. He is now playing for a mediocre team. You know why? He can't get along with people. He cannot get along with his fellow teammates. I'm not trying to rip this young man because I'm praying for his salvation. This young man, who claims to be a Christian, should stop being rebellious and full of himself. You need to join a team and be decisive to stay there. You need to be joined to a husband and a wife and stay there. An unbroken covenant brings life and prosperity. An unbroken covenant means you keep your word. It means you stay there even though you don't like her anymore. You stay with him even though you don't love him anymore.

Psalm 1:1-3 "Blessed is the man who walks not in the counsel of the ungodly, nor stands in the path of sinners, nor sits in the seat of the scornful; but his delight is in the law of the Lord, and in His law he meditates day and night. He shall be like a tree planted by the rivers of water. That brings forth its fruit in its season, whose leaf also shall not wither; and whatever he does shall prosper."

Jesus said in **John 15:5**, "I am the vine, you are the branches. He who abides [or if you continue] in Me, and I in him, bears much fruit; for without me you can do nothing." Verse 7 says, "If you abide in Me, and my words abide in you, you will ask what you desire, and it shall be done for you." You might say, "Well pastor,

I've asked for a lot of things and I haven't gotten it!" If you're really abiding in Him, you only ask for what He puts in your heart in the first place.

Some people say, "Well, you know once you're saved, you're always saved or you never got saved." Here's another possibility. **Colossians 1:21-23** "And you, who once were alienated and enemies in your mind by wicked works, yet now he has reconciled... In the body of His flesh through death, to present you holy, and blameless, and above reproach in His sight – if indeed you continue [in the covenant] in the faith, grounded and steadfast, and are not moved away from the hope of the gospel which you heard, which was preached to every creature under Heaven."

Why would the Holy Spirit say, "be moved away," if it was impossible to move away? (Also read **Galatians 5:21)**

Life Lesson: Prosperity comes only by obedience to the covenant.

Deuteronomy 29:9 "Therefore keep the words of this covenant, and do them, that you may prosper in all that you do." I believe God wants to prosper everybody with peace, with love and joy, provision. I didn't say to have five Rolls Royce and eight Rolexes and three airplanes. No, that's called greed. I believe God wants you to have enough and more than enough to give to somebody else. Prosperity is for distribution, not accumulation. Prosperity is to bless somebody else. It's not to live high on the hog!

God wants to prosper His people so they can establish His covenant on the earth. **Deuteronomy 8:18** "And you shall remember the Lord your God, for it is

He who gives you power to get wealth, that He may establish His covenant which He swore to your fathers, as it is this day." In the new covenant, God wants to establish the Great commission **Matthew 28:18-20**.

God will bless businessman and business women when you work so that you can have wealth to preach the Great Commission and to win people to Jesus. When people look at you and they see you are prosperous, you have all your needs met, you're not living from check to check and they say, "Man, what do you have?" I'm obeying the covenant. I'm doing my best to obey Jesus. I love God and choose not to leave because this guarantees a blessing. The purpose of prosperity, therefore, is to help others who have needs, fulfill the Great Commission, fulfill our own personal assignments, and live an overflowing, abundant life!

A broken covenant brings drastic consequences not only for the covenant breaker but for his family and community. You can read all these scriptures later but **Joshua 7:11, 20-21** talks about Achan. In Joshua 6 they had defeated a strong city called Jericho. Somebody in the camp broke covenant. God had said don't take any of their money, any of their stuff and a guy named Achan took stuff and as a result they lost. Broken covenants have long term effects.

Malachi 3:8-10 "Will a man rob God? Yet you have robbed Me! But you say, 'In what way have we robbed You?' In tithes and offerings. You are cursed with a curse, for you have robbed Me." Does God put a curse on you if you don't tithe? No, if you don't tithe you're under the curse of the world. You will be much more blessed if you give God what is His.

Exodus 20:5 says, "You shall not bow down to them

nor serve them. For I, the Lord your God, am a jealous God, visiting the iniquity of the fathers upon the children to the third and fourth generations." Sin reproduces in your children.

I once heard John Maxwell say, "You teach what you know, but you reproduce what you are." The acorn doesn't fall far from the tree. If you yell at your wife, if you don't submit to your husband, if you tell your kid, "It's the boss, tell him I'm not here," you have just taught your kid to lie. Don't be surprised when she's seventeen and lies to you. You broke covenant and now she's going to break covenant and make your life miserable.

1 Corinthians 6:18 "Flee sexual immorality. Every sin that a man does is outside the body, but he who commits sexual immorality sins against his own body." How do you sin against your own body? Two ways, it creates in you an insatiable desire to have sex and secondly, when you get married you will always have soul ties to your previous lovers. **Genesis 34:1-3**

2 Corinthians 6:14-18 "Do not be unequally yoked with unbelievers. For what fellowship has righteousness with lawlessness? And what communion has light with darkness?" Don't date or go out with an unbeliever.

Don't you ever go in business with an unsaved person. Don't ever have a roommate who's unsaved. You will bring a curse on yourself and everybody who thought you were a Christian is now going to be talking behind your back because you are playing the hypocrite.

For the many in the church who have this insatiable desire to live with somebody before they get married, first of all, you're in fornication and you will not go to Heaven. If you die when you're living with a man or woman, you will go to hell. You need to get married or you need to break up. I tell you that in all the love of a father. You're breaking covenant and you know what the family is thinking? Hypocrites! (Hebrews 13:4)

The decree of the first covenant. Decree means to declare or speak. **Genesis 1:28** "Then God blessed them, and God said to them, 'Be fruitful and multiply; fill the earth and subdue it; have dominion over the fish of the sea, over the birds of the air, and over every living thing that moves on earth.'"

The Decree of the First Covenant

This decree was given to Adam and Eve. Adam was to have dominion over the plants and the animals etc. He was to be fruitful, multiply, subdue the earth, and exercise dominion. When they sinned, God reestablished a covenant with them, killed an animal, covered their nakedness with fur, and then he tells the devil in **Genesis 3:15** one day a seed is going to come from this woman. You will bruise His heel but He will crush your head and the devil's been trying to figure out that seed ever since. It was given to Adam and it was lost by Adam and Eve in Genesis 3. It was reconfirmed to Noah in **Genesis 9**.

From Noah, it was given to Abraham the father of our faith. Abraham was a pagan. Don't ask me why God chose him. That's between him and God. He says to Abraham, who fathered the nation of Israel, in **Genesis 12:1**, "Now the Lord had said to Abraham, 'Get out of your country, from your family and from your father's house, to a land that I will show you. I will make you a great nation; I will bless you and make your name great; and you shall be a blessing. I will bless those who bless you, and I will curse him who curses you."

My friend, don't make a mistake in your daily life and in your conversation to curse Israel. God loves the Palestinians; but He'll bless the people of Israel. In **Genesis 17**, verse five onward, He reconfirms that to Abraham again and then from Abraham it was restated to Israel. The covenant was given to Israel. Pray that our country recognizes this fact.

Exodus 19:5-6 "'Now therefore, if you [Israel] will indeed obey My voice and keep My covenant, then you shall be a special treasure to Me above all people; for all the earth is Mine. And you shall be to Me a Kingdom of priests and a holy nation.' These are the words which you shall speak to the children of Israel." Israel failed. The Church, by the way, does not replace Israel. God has a plan for Israel.

It was made again to David, King David. **2 Samuel 7:16-17** "'[David] your house and your Kingdom shall be established forever before you. Your throne shall be established forever.' According to all these words and according to all this vision, so Nathan spoke to David."

That means we're going to see David ruling back on the earth during the Millennial Reign of Christ. It was reestablished and won by Jesus. Jesus won the covenant that Adam lost. It says in **Hebrews 9:11-17**, "But Christ came as High Priest of the good things." When you sing you are good, He's the high priest of the good things to come. "With the greater and more perfect tabernacle not made with hands, that is, not of this creation. Not with the blood of goats and calves, but with His own blood He entered the Most Holy Place once for all, having obtained eternal redemption." Jesus doesn't have to die again. "For if the blood of bulls and goats and the ashes of a heifer, sprinkling the unclean, sanctifies for the purifying of the flesh, how much more shall the blood of Christ, who through the eternal Spirit offered Himself without spot to God, cleanse your conscience from dead works to serve the living God?"

Jesus can clean you up. Verses 15-18, "And for this reason He is the Mediator of the new covenant, by means of death, for the redemption of the transgressions under the first covenant, that those who are called may receive the promise of the eternal inheritance. For where there is a testament, there must also of necessity be the death of the testator. For a testament is in force after men are dead, since it has no power at all while the testator lives. Therefore, not even the first covenant was dedicated without blood."

Hebrews 12:24 "To Jesus the Mediator of the new covenant, and to the blood of sprinkling that speaks better things." You see we should have better things. We have a better covenant. Of course you know **Matthew 28:18-20**, the Great Commission is part of the new covenant. You can't separate them. "And Jesus came and spoke to them, saying, 'All authority has been given to Me in Heaven and on earth. Go therefore and make disciples of all the nations, baptizing them in the name of the Father and of the Son and of the Holy Spirit, teaching them to observe all things that I have commanded you; and lo, I am with you always, even to the end of the age.' Amen."

In our time that means the whole Bible.

This covenant was given to the Church to establish on earth. Jesus is the head of the Church. Jesus is over all of the devil's principalities and powers and he gave that power to the church. **Ephesians 1:17** and onwards,

"That the God of our Lord Jesus Christ, the Father of glory, may give to you the spirit of wisdom and revelation in the knowledge of Him," What wisdom? We have a covenant. "The eyes of your understanding being enlightened; that you may know what is the hope of His calling, what are the riches of the glory of His inheritance in the saints, and what is the exceeding greatness of His power toward us who believe. According to the working of His mighty power which He worked in Christ when He raised Him from the dead and seated Him at His right hand in the Heavenly places, far above all principality and power and might and dominion, and every name that is named, not only in this age but also in that which is to come. And He put all things under His feet, and gave Him to be head over all things to the church." **Ephesians 1:18-22**

If everything is under the feet and we're part of Jesus as the Church then everything is under our feet. "Which is His body, the fullness of Him who fills all in all."

Life Lesson: Every time you take communion, you are restating your allegiance to Jesus and the new covenant which includes not only thanking Him for your salvation, but your decision to be a part of the Great Commission. Every time you take communion you are restating your pledge of allegiance to God.

The Details of the Covenant

There are details of the covenant. I want you to understand that there are five aspects of biblical covenant that will unlock your biblical understanding because as Westerners we generally don't understand it.

Supremacy

First of all, let's look at supremacy and its importance. Supremacy means that God is above and surpasses all others. Jesus is far above every fallen angel; every demon; every politician; every earthy ruler; including the coming anti-Christ world ruler; and above the globalists/illuminati agenda **Ephesians 1:21-23** Nobody is above Him. You serve "numero uno." You might not be anything by yourself, but in Him, we can do all things. God is supreme and surpasses all others.

Ephesians 1:21-23 "far above all principality and power and might and dominion, and every name that is named, not only in this age but also in that which is to come." And He put all **things** under His feet, and gave Him **to be** head over all **things** to the church, which is His body, the fullness of Him who fills all in all."

Secondly, He shows supremacy as creator, redeemer, and when He speaks directly to others. That's amazing; He's big enough to make the universe and small enough to speak right in your heart.

Thirdly, when we discover the full requirements and implications of His supremacy, we will immediately see whether we have been treating God too casually or not seeking after Him as we should in a loving and respectful relationship. It's amazing how we use the word God. Some people say God as a cuss word. Others just flippantly say, "Oh God!" You even hear people hit their thumb with a hammer and yell: "Jesus!" Be careful how you use the name God. Don't treat Him too lightly. We should have a somber reverence for God, We must have respect.

Proverbs 9:10 "The fear of the Lord is the beginning

of wisdom, and the knowledge of the Holy One is understanding." You want to get understanding? Get a fear of God.

Hebrews 7:26 "For such a High Priest was fitting for us, who is holy, harmless, undefiled, separate from sinners, and has become higher than the Heavens."

Look at that scripture again. I want to be holy. I want to be harmless. I want to be undefiled. I want to be separate from sin. I want to be like Jesus my high priest. How about you? Here's test: time. I promise you that on that day He's going to say, "I saw how you answered." Answering the following questions gives us a clue as to how we are living our lives in relationship to His supremacy. Are you ready?

Am I living in obedience to His written word (that means the Bible), and the revealed word which the Holy Spirit speaks directly to you in a "still small voice"? **1 Kings 19:126**

The Holy Spirit says, "Go and forgive him," and you say, "I'm not going to forgive him. That's not the way I am." This is when you must deny self-will. The Holy Spirit will help you. Ask yourself: "Am I living in self-denial? Do I put His preferences, His call above mine? Am I an overcomer by totally submitting to His will? Is the plant Kingdom dominating me because I am bound to smoking? Am I bound by drugs or alcohol?"

I can do all things through Christ who strengthens me. Am I a bondservant to Christ? A bondservant was a slave that was set free who chose to come, out of love for his master, to work for him again. Am I a bondservant to Christ or do I exercise my new won freedom and choices? Am I saved, but consistently do what I want to do? "And He died for all, that those who live should live no longer for themselves, but for Him who died for them and rose again." **2 Corinthians 5:15**

Are you bearing the fruit of the spirit? I didn't ask you if you believe in love, joy, gentleness, and self-control. I asked you if you're living it.

Stewardship

The second axiom or principle of covenant is stewardship. We have an obligation to others as God's stewards, or managers, of the gospel. Many believers think salvation is only about their own destiny and afterlife. Forget the size of the mansion; it's how many other people did you help bring up there. **John 14:2**

Christians are stewards of His delegated authority. It means He gave you authority and as an ambassador of Christ we demonstrate Kingdom power and the Word of Godto other people. We don't just talk it; we show it. We lay hands on people right smack in the middle of Walmart. Hey, Muslims will pray in the middle of an airport; why don't we? Instead of saying, "Oh no, I have a contageous disease," speak to that disease and command it to die in Jesus' name!

2 Corinthians 5:19-20 talks about that we are ambassadors of Christ. **Matthew 28:19** says "Go!" He said "Go!" He'll tell you when to stop, and when to go. Some Christians need to get out of their comfor zones and go and do something. Jesus said in **John 20:21**, "Peace to you! As the Father has sent Me, I also send you." That's part of the covenant.

Stipulations

Thirdly, there are stipulations. We all function under

certain stipulations. What does stipulation mean? These are ethical and behavioral requirements of the covenant. These ethical stipulations are necessary because there are always certain behaviors that the King expects from those who pledge allegiance to serve Him in return for His benefits.

We have been given hundreds of commands to obey in order to live out our Christian lives such as **Galatians 5:16-16** and **Ephesians 5:1 all the way to 6:8.** This whole concept is contrary to our current post-modern, wishy-washy, relativistic climate in which we have turned the Ten Commandments into the ten suggestions for a better life. Many people want Jesus to be their Savior, but He must be Lord!

You may have heard the phrase, "Accept Jesus as your personal Savior." However, the word "Savior" is used 64 times in the Bible while "Lord" is used 7,234 times in the Old Testament and 712 times in the New Testament for a total of 7,946 times, therefore "Lord" is more important to God than "Savior." Please understand, if He's not your Lord, He is not your Savior.

Romans 10:9 says that if you confess Jesus as Lord and believe that He was raised from the dead you will be saved. Confess Jesus as Lord.

Sanctions

Fourthly, there are sanctions. When Vladimir Putin and the Premier of Russia invaded the Ukraine, President Obama and the whole world said, "We're going to put sanctions on you." What's a sanction? A sanction is an economic boycott. There are consequences of either obedience and/or disobedience. Everybody wants to go to Heaven; but nobody wants consequences. If you were an athlete, football or basketball, you know all those drills they call "suicides." Your guts are coming out of your mouth, you catch them and bring them back in! But when you are playing the other team and it's the fourth quarter and you beat them by twenty-five points you know why, because you play like you practice and you will live your life the way you pray and obey.

A large percentage of Believers have the false notion that God is merely a giver of blessings. They believe that there are no consequences for sin because we are no longer held by the works of the law, but justified by grace.

But grace says in **Romans 6:1-2**, "Shall we continue in sin that grace may abound?" God forbid and **Titus 2:11-13** will tell you what grace is all about, "For the grace of God that brings salvation has appeared to all men teaching us that denying ungodliness and worldly lusts we should live soberly, righteously, and godly in this present age. Looking for the blessed hope and glorious appearance of our great God and Savior Jesus Christ."

Some preachers will have you believe in hyper-grace. I tell you what grace teaches you – live right and have sanctions in your life. Jude 4 says that some people falsely believe that the grace of God is a license to live in sin. Consequently, America, England, and Canada are being flooded with positive self-help messages with no mention of repentance, hell, and the judgment that comes from failing to adhere to God's sanctions. There are going to be a lot of people in hell looking for preachers to ask them, "Why didn't you tell me the truth?" Do you know that most preachers are insecure? Most preachers are approval junkies. They stand by the door for you to shake their hand and say, "That was a wonderful sermon Reverend so and so." They should respond, "Thank you. All the glory goes to God."

Personally, I want people to know I love them. I also love them enough to tell them the truth in love. I want to see them serving God. I want to quote an old missionary, Charles Greenway. He once told me, "You know Garcia. In the old days we had a lot of negative preaching. We had a lot of negative preaching, but we had positive living. Now, you have positive preaching and negative living." I never forgot that.

We must learn that we can experience complete forgiveness for a sin, but we must deal with the consequences of that sin; for example, God forgives the adulterer. But then that person has to deal with the enormous consequences of that broken covenant. He's got to look his daughter in the eye when she says, "Daddy, why did you run off with a girl that's only two years older than me?" Adultery has got a lot of consequences.

Succession

Here is something we never consider. John Maxwell says, "We teach what we know, but we reproduce what we are." Somebody is watching you. Somebody is watching your Christianity. How will my decisions affect them? God expects all Believers to serve Him with a plan for their successive multiple generations. You are not in this alone. It's not us three and no more. Somebody is watching you. You are affecting somebody. You will leave a legacy; it's either good or bad. But in our post-modern, relativistic mentality, we often make decisions based on what we see and what we desire at the moment. Relativism means truth lies in the eyes of the beholder and changes according to the situation. That's not true. Truth is consistent. We have a habit of making decisions based upon desires, emotions, influence, and what's popular.

However, every time a major decision in life is made regarding family, church, ministry, business, or community, we should be conscious of how it will affect the present and succeeding generations. Your kids and your grandchildren are watching. Perhaps you say, "Man, I'm fifteen, I don't have any kids." Yes, but your schoolmates are watching you. The Millennial Christian must especially realize this because the Millennial Generation (those born from 1980–2000) tend to value authenticity extremely high.

Some of your friends may go to hell or Heaven depending on how you act. "Well, I have nothing to do with that!" Yes, you do; you are the salt of the earth and you are an ambassador. Don't lead them to hell. Ask yourself, "How have my decisions and behavior affected my family and relationships? What about the church I attend?" Some people say all churches are the same; no, they are not! Some churches will take you straight to hell. Many churches are preaching a message that contradicts God's Word or they preach a watered down gospel with positive, uplifting messages without any conviction of sin, without any holiness.

Then there is the subject of divorce. Some woman might say, "Well, I just don't love your father anymore." As a result your sons, your daughters, are crippled for the rest of their lives.

What about indebtedness. "Well, we'll just charge it!" Really? All your credit cards are charged to the max because you didn't know how to say no. What about your choice of career or job? I once met a young woman, this is serious business, who told me, "God led me to be a strip-teaser." I said, "How would you feel if I told you he led me to be a murderer?" "Oh no! You can't do that!" I said, "Neither can you do that."

What about your choice of where you live? You might say, "Well, we'll just live anywhere." Don't just live anywhere. You need to discern where God wants you to go through prayer. Make a choice to pray about your decisions and make sure they line up to the Word of God. **James 3:17**

It is absolutely imperative that we apply the Kingdom concept of covenant and apply it to our daily living.

CHAPTER FOUR

Jesus Secured Victory Over Satan

"Having disarmed principalities and powers, He made a public spectacle of them, triumphing over them in it." **Colossians 2:15**

"When a strong man, fully armed, guards his own palace, his goods are in peace. But when a stronger than he comes upon him and overcomes him, he takes from him all his armor in which he trusted, and divides his spoils." **Luke 11:21-22**

"Inasmuch then as the children have partaken of flesh and blood, He Himself likewise shared in the same, that through death He might destroy him who had the power of death, that is, the devil," **Hebrews 2:14**

"In which you once walked according to the course of this world, according to the prince of the power of the air, the spirit who now works in the sons of disobedience," **Ephesians 2:2**

"That the God of our Lord Jesus Christ, the Father of glory, may give to you the spirit of wisdom and revelation in the knowledge of Him, the eyes of your understanding being enlightened; that you may know what is the hope of His calling, what are the riches of the glory of His inheritance in the saints, and what is the exceeding greatness of His power toward us who believe, according to the working of His mighty power which He worked in Christ when He raised Him from the dead and seated Him at His right hand in the Heavenly places, far above all principality and power and might and dominion, and every name that is named, not only in this age but also in that which is to come. And He put all things under His feet, and gave Him to be head over all things to the church, which is His body, the fullness of Him who fills all in all." **Ephesians 1:17-23**

Key Take Away: At the cross and by the resurrection, Jesus secured victory over Satan and his allies in the air but each of us must now apply that victory.

We are in a war whether you realize it or not. As far as God is concerned, there is only the Kingdom of God and the Kingdom of Satan. That's all He's concerned with. You need to know that the devil is doing everything he can for you to join him in hell, in the Lake of Fire, for all of eternity. At the same time, God is doing everything He can so that we can go with Him in the Kingdom of Heaven.

The Kingdom of God is when Heaven invades the earth through the life of a faithful believer and brings the characteristics of Heaven here on earth. Where there is sickness, He brings healing. Where there is poverty, He brings provision. Where there is confusion, He brings wisdom. The Kingdom of God, the Bible tells us in Luke 17, is within us. As we have reviewed, the Kingdom of God is God's rulership over your life. Is God's government in your life? People say, "Well, I believe in the Kingdom of God." Yes, but who's the boss of your life?

If you're the boss, you know not the Kingdom.

The Kingdom of God is the rulership of God and the government of God operating in and through our lives. Not only does He rule us, but we rule demon powers because of His rulership. Not only does He rule us, but we rule over every situation that confronts us. That's the Kingdom of God and a lot of the Church have only entered the Kingdom. We've been stuck in the hallway. We're born again, but we've never moved out from there. This may come as a shock to you, but Jesus came preaching the gospel of the Kingdom, not just the cross. The cross and the blood, I thank God for it. It is the entrance into the Kingdom but from then on let's remove the Kingdom of darkness and bring Heaven's influence down to Earth!

You're going to find out the tremendous victory that Jesus achieved, but just because He achieved it, doesn't mean you will walk in that victory. You've got to take it, believe it, apply it, and fight with it. Salvation is available to everybody, but not everybody is going to take it. The giving is God's, but the taking is ours.

We are in a conflict; we're in a war. You don't have a problem with your mother-in-law; you have a problem with the Kingdom of Satan. You don't have a problem with unemployment; you have a problem with the Kingdom of darkness that's robbing you from being a provider for your home. Every problem you have is a spiritual problem. We must look at how the Kingdom of God rules and how the Kingdom of Satan rules because you can't take people out of the Kingdom of darkness unless you first understand how the Kingdom of God operates. I can't bring people into the Kingdom that I know unless I know how the Kingdom of God operates. Did you know that today, many churches are impotent? We're going to find out why many churches don't make people disciples of Jesus. It's because they're too busy fighting among themselves. Jesus said a Kingdom divided against itself cannot stand. How does the Kingdom of God rule? How does it operate?

Relationship

First of all, He rules through relationship. This is a key word. That means whatever God does in His Kingdom, other people are critically important. I often hear people say, "I love Jesus; I just can't stand church. I don't like church people." Well, you don't understand the Kingdom. You don't have to like us; you have to love us. God's Kingdom works through relationships. He's not going to give to anybody or any church all wisdom and knowledge. He makes it so that we need one another.

Secondly, God rules through fatherhood. **1 John 3:1-2** reads: "Behold what manner of love the Father has bestowed on us, that we should be called children of God!"

You're a child of God. Please place as secondary your earthly identity. If you're saved, according to **Ephesians 2**, your citizenship is in Heaven. Everything else is secondary. It says, "Therefore the world does not know us, because it did not know Him. Beloved, now we are children of God; and it has not yet been revealed what we shall be." If you don't like somebody in the Kingdom, you just don't see what God sees. You need to see them as someone whom Christ died for; and see the potential of that brother or sister. Pray for the Father to show you their potential; not the obvious. It is easy to see the obvious. Satan magnifies the obvious; God magnifies what's unseen. He magnifies their potential.

Satan will magnify their past and their present; God magnifies their potential and their future.

If the Word says, "It has not yet been revealed what we shall be," don't judge anybody until the end. **1 John 3:2** "But we know that when He is revealed, we shall be like Him, for we shall see Him as He is." That means everybody who is truly born again is going to be like Jesus. All the wrinkles are going to be ironed out.

Never view your Heavenly Father through the eyeglasses of your human father. Don't look at your Heavenly father through all of the frailties and the faults of the natural father you had because if you do and your father was cruel, you'll think God is cruel and Satan has robbed you. You need to view your Heavenly Father through the eyeglasses of the Word of God. Let the Word of Godtell you who your Heavenly Father is. We have a great, loving Father.

God rules through fatherhood. There's a song by Rick Pino that I happen to love very much called "Dove's Eyes"[24] and it says, "I love Your face, I love Your kisses, I love Your embrace, I love Your presence."

When you know the Father like I do, you will love that song and even though I'm a man's man, I love His kisses. I love it! My father never did that with me. I have many sons: in the natural, I have one, but spiritually, I have a lot and I kiss every one of them. God rules through fatherhood. God gives His children identity. You might be the lowest of the lows. You may homeless. You might be nothing but a strung-out junkie, but if you come to Jesus your Father, He becomes your King of kings and the Lord of lords.

Immediately, you're translated, according to

Colossians 1:13, from the Kingdom of darkness to the Kingdom of His dear Son, Jesus. Immediately, you have status. Immediately, you are important. Immediately, you have dignity. Immediately, you have worth. You are not junk in the eyes of God. God sent His Son to die for us and He didn't send His Son to die for junk because when His blood cleanses you, you become so valuable to the Kingdom. He gives you identity.

Galatians 4:6-7 says: "And because you are sons, God has sent forth the Spirit of His Son into your hearts, crying out, 'Abba, Father!' Therefore, you are no longer a slave but a son, and if a son, then an heir of God through Christ." God rules through fatherhood.

He gives His children identity and God gives each of His children the following things. He gives affirmation. There is a difference between admiration and affirmation. Every wife and every husband needs three things. Every son and daughter needs three things. Which means everybody needs three things.

Admiration. Admiration is when you thank somebody for what they've done. Gratefulness and thankfulness have power. Of the ten lepers, one came back to say thank you and he got completely healed. That's another message. Admiration is when you say, "Honey, thank you for cooking." "Baby, you thank me every day." "And you keep cooking for me." Thank you for fixing the car. Thank you for being a provider of the house. Thank you, son, you did well. There is power in admiration; God made us that way.

Affirmation. Affirmation is different. Admiration is when you thank somebody for what they've done. Affirmation is when you thank them for who they are. In other words, "Come here, son. I love you because

86

you are my son." Or "Come here daughter. I love you because you are my daughter." "I love you because you are kind."

In **Matthew 3:17**, when Jesus got baptized, suddenly a voice came from Heaven saying, "This is my beloved Son in whom I am well pleased." Jesus hadn't begun His ministry yet, but the Father was pleased in Him. I've often wondered, why did Jesus need to be baptized?

One of the reasons is because the world needed to hear that the Father was pleased in Him and the power of affirmation will keep your marriage together. The power of affirmation will keep your son, even though he may run around with his friends, he'll come back. Your daughter will come back. The prodigal daughters and sons will come back because they know that mom and dad are affirming them instead of rejecting them. We need to affirm more.

Affection. Everybody needs affection. It's not just a girl thing that we embrace and kiss; it's a guy thing. As a father, as a mother, as a brother or sister, not in a lustful way.

God rules through fatherhood. He gives His children identity. In identity the Father gives us affirmation and He gives us correction. **Hebrews 12:5-11** in the English Standard Version says, "And have you forgotten the exhortation that addresses you as sons? 'My son, do not regard lightly the discipline of the Lord, nor be weary when reproved by him. For the Lord disciplines the one he loves, and chastises every son whom he receives.'"

Have you felt His discipline recently? If you have, it proves that you are a daughter or a son. I've actually met people who have said, "I've never felt God's discipline!"

And I say, "Well, I invite you to be saved right now. Repeat after me." "No, no I've been in church all my life!" If you've never received His discipline, you don't belong to Him. God loves you, but you're not a son. He loves you as a sinner, but not as a son. Stop complaining when you are going through trials. Learn the difference and discern the difference and you'll have a chance to see more of that between the devil's tempting's and God's pruning's and God's disciplines.

God's Nutrition

God gives you two kinds of food. He gives milk and He gives meat. Milk is for the babies in the Lord. Milk is the *logos*. Milk is the written word. A baby in the Lord, this is what he gets. He's not going to understand much else. He'll hardly understand this. You don't give beef stew to a newborn. The problem is some people have been newborn for 47 years!!

1 Peter 2:2-3 says: "As newborn babes, desire the pure milk of the word that you may grow thereby, if indeed you have tasted that the Lord is gracious."

If you are really saved, you will be hungry. What do you think of a baby that never wants to eat? He is sick! She's going to die! I'm amazed people say, "Oh my husband came forward and accepted the Lord, but he never reads his Bible." Perhaps he really didn't get saved. Well, what did he do? He came forward, but he did not repent, then he went back to his old ways. If you're saved, you're hungry for the Bible. If you're saved, we've got to kick you out of church. If you're saved, you're here early and you leave late. If you're saved, you have an appetite. You can't wait to eat.

You don't care if a five-year old is preaching; you're

going to get something out of it. You're starving! You can't wait to get more. It's time to get mature in God. If you don't understand the written word, what are you going to do when you get to the meat of the word which is the *rhema*. *Rhema* is the quickened word, the inspired word. *Rhema* is when God can talk to you and say, "Today, you're going to meet somebody and I want you to be ready to witness to them." That is a direct word from God. You say, "Well that's never happened to me." That's because you're still drinking milk or you haven't recognized that it was God.

Hebrews 5:12-14 reads: "For though by this time you ought to be teachers, you need someone to teach you again the first principles of the oracles of God.

You have come to need milk and not solid food. For everyone who partakes only of milk is unskilled in the word of righteousness, for he is a babe. But solid food," solid food is the *rhema*. Solid food is inspired word from the Holy Spirit to you specifically. That's when he tells you, "I want you to go to the ministry fair and I want you to join this ministry." Also, "I want you to ask for forgiveness." "But solid food belongs to those who are of full age, that is, those who by reason of use have their [spiritual] senses exercised to discern both good and evil." You know you are on solid food when you can sense good and evil without trying it.

The world says, "Don't knock it 'til you try it." Solid food says, "Don't try it 'til you discern it." **Luke 8:18** says "Therefore take heed how you hear [or your attitude when hearing or reading God's Word]. For whoever has [obedience to that Word], to him more [understanding and revelation] will be given; and whoever does not have [obedience], even what he seems to have will be taken from him." In other words, obedience to the written Word of God(logos) qualifies one to receive the living Word (rhema): the specific, personal revelation from God.

Revelation

He has a relationship through revelation. The Kingdom rules through revelation. He wants to reveal to each and every one of us what is your purpose on planet earth and what are your assignments. I am in my divine purpose. It's hard to understand somebody unless you can discern what their assignment is.

I want to go deeper into revelation. The Kingdom of God rules through revelation. Has anybody ever died and you really believed God for their healing? They died and you just didn't understand? There was a little five-year-old that used to bring his daddy up to the altars. He used to love my preaching even though he was a little kid. Yet he still died of massive cancer in the brain. I prayed for him, I laid hands on him. God gave him two more years.

I received peace when I discovered **Deuteronomy 29:29**. Please absorb this: "The secret things belong to the Lord our God, but those things which are revealed belong to us and our children forever, that they may do all the words of this law." That means that there are secret things that as long as we are on this world we will never understand. Don't force God or get angry at God to tell you why when it's a secret thing. You stay and do the revealed things. Look at it again, "But those things which are revealed," who do they belong to? Us. Focus on the revealed things and then pass that revelation on to your children. Revelation was meant to be passed on.

That's why we have such trouble with our kids, because we don't have enough revelation.

Ephesians 1:17 reads: "That the God of our Lord Jesus Christ, the Father of glory, may give to you the spirit of wisdom and revelation in the knowledge of Him." Why would the Holy Spirit tell Paul to write that? It's God's will for you not to be in the dark. For every problem, for every door that is locked, there is a revelation that will unlock that door. Regardless if it's business, marriage, or anything. There is a revelation waiting for you and most of it has already been written in God's almighty book – the Word of God.

There are two things about revelation. First of all, it's not just knowledge, but revealed knowledge. Or a *rhema*, a *rhema* from God. What's a *rhema* from God? *Rhema* means a specific word to a specific person about a specific thing for a specific time. It's for you. It's when you're reading Ezekiel and He's talking to you. Has that ever happened to you?

You're reading, "Don't put new wine in old wineskins" and all of a sudden the Holy Spirit says, "You know what, you're getting real traditional. I can't do what I want to do in you because you are stuck in your thinking." You say, "God just spoke to me!" That's a *rhema*. You will only get that when you obey the *logos*. No *logos*, no *rhema*.

When people disobey the *logos*, the devil will twist the *rhema* and he will deceive you into thinking God led you when He didn't lead you. Case in point – a guy in business, and the Bible says, "Don't be unequally yoked with an unbeliever," but he's dead set to go into business with this unsaved guy, no matter what.

She's determined to marry this guy, even though he's a heathen and all of a sudden she says, "I feel a witness in my spirit. I feel a confirmation – he's going to become a Christian."

God's not going to go against His written word. *Rhema* will never contradict *logos*. What happens when you're disobedient and you're rebellious and you're in control of your life and you're dead set on having your own way? The devil will twist it and give you what is called strange peace. You will feel good about your rebellion. "I feel good about it! There's nothing you could say to talk me out of it!" My job is not to talk you out of it; my job is to tell you the warning of the consequences of your disobedience. (see **Deuteronomy 29:19**)

Jesus healed all who came to Him. **Matthew 8:16-17** everybody that came to Jesus got healed but on specific occasions He received specific revelation to heal a certain person out of a multitude. Why is this important? If you want to move in the gifts of the spirit, you need to learn how to flow in *rhema*. Do you remember the cripple by the pool of Bethesda?

John 5:1-3 "After this there was a feast of the Jews, and Jesus went up to Jerusalem. Now there is in Jerusalem by the Sheep Gate a pool, which is called in Hebrew, Bethesda, having five porches. In these lay a great multitude," in the Greek the word multitude is how many people you can see in one glance. That means there were thousands out there. "Sick people, blind, lame, paralyzed, waiting for the moving of the water." I'll jump to verse 5, "Now a certain man was there who had an infirmity thirty-eight years. When Jesus saw him lying there, and knew that he already had been in that condition a long time, He said to him,

'Do you want to be made well?' The sick man answered Him, 'Sir, I have no man to put me into the pool when the water is stirred up; but while I am coming, another steps down before me.' Jesus said to him, 'Rise, take up your bed and walk.'"

I'm not going to reason with you. I came here to get you healed. I heard a *rhema* from my Father. "And immediately the man was made well, took up his bed, and walked. And that day was the Sabbath." I want to ask you something, was he the only sick person there? Why did He heal only that man? He had a direct word from His Father. Great miracles happen with *rhema*. Learn to hear the *rhema*.

The same example is in **Luke 7:11-17** "Now it happened, the day after, that He went into a city called Nain;" I was actually there when I went to Israel the last time. Nain's just a little hole in the wall, just a little place. This is the only time Jesus went to Nain. There was a large crowd there, I am going to paraphrase now you can read that on your own, and they were carrying a boy. They were having a funeral procession for a boy. The Jews bury you within 24 hours. Jesus goes up to the boy and says, "Young man, I say to you, arise," and the kid got up. He stopped the whole funeral procession. That who was dead is now alive. Everybody's jumping for joy and they said in verse 16, "God has visited His people." I want to ask you a question: was he the only dead person in Nain at that time? Weren't there other sick people? Why didn't Jesus go around to the others? Why only one? The bottom line: It was a word from God.

Mark 7:24-30, the Syro-Phoenician women, this Greek woman had a demon possessed daughter. She lives in Sidon in Tyre, that's Lebanon. The Father tells

Him, "Son, I want you to go to Lebanon." I can just see Him, "Ok, I'll just go." As Jesus walked, so you walk. When He inspires you to do something, you do it. He goes there and some woman says, "Thou son of David! Have mercy on me!" You know the rest of the story, He says, "Go! I've never seen such faith in all of Israel!" And at that very moment, the girl was set free from demons. Why no one else? It was a direct word from God. What am I telling you? Learn to obey this *logos* but be open to the Holy Spirit when He gives you a *rhema*. Most people have cheated themselves out of a miracle because rhemas are unusual.

Rhemas don't make sense sometimes. You want me to leave this revival and go to Lebanon? God, they need me here. Do what He says! You want me to stop everything and go to Nain? That's in the opposite direction. Yes, there's a boy I want to raise from the dead. You can do the works of Jesus, **John 14:12** if you hear the *rhema* from God. God's looking for people who are going to be obedient and hear the spoken *rhema* word of God. But if you're just disobedient to the written word, you are not ever going to listen to the spoken word because the spoken word doesn't make sense.

One time the Lord told Jesus, "Spit in that guy's eye!" **Mark 8:23; Mark 5:1-8** WHAT? Another time He said, "Just speak to him." You understand what I'm saying? That's why you can't just nail Jesus down. Do I spit on Him? Do I lay hands on them? Do I talk to them? Do I slap them? You know he told Smith Wigglesworth, "Kick them! Punch them!"

You and I can bring the miraculous through the general revelation of the written word. Understand what I'm writing, you can bring miracles just with the written Bible. But mighty signs and wonders come when we received a *rhema* for a specific person. You remember the man at the Gate Beautiful? Alms, alms. Peter and John come walking. I mean it was the third hour. They went there every day at the third hour. Alms, alms. Sometimes they gave and sometimes they didn't. But one day he said alms and Peter got hit with the Holy Spirit. He said, "Silver and gold, I have none. But such as I have, I give to you. In the name of Jesus rise up and walk." And the guy got up! **Acts 3:1-8** There were other beggars there. Why him? I don't know. It was a *rhema* from God and it will bypass your natural reasoning.

Your reasoning will say, "Lord, this man's been a cripple all his life. His muscles have atrophied. They just don't move anymore." When God gives you a *rhema*, I don't care what it is; do it! It doesn't make sense, but make sure it's God because it will never contradict the Word of God. If you're young and inexperienced, make sure you have the witness of your elders and your pastors. If you tell me the Lord has led you to the next moon trip, I probably will speak to you.

Acts 14:8-10 says: "And in Lystra a certain man without strength in his feet was sitting, a cripple from his mother's womb, who had never walked. This man heard Paul speaking. Paul, observing him intently and seeing that he had faith to be healed, said with a loud voice, 'Stand up straight on your feet!' And he leaped and walked." The same thing with Peter in Lydda (**Acts 9:32-35**) he sees a man named Aeneas and he healed him. Why the miraculous? People know how to apply the written word and they know how to apply the *rhema* spoken word.

Resignation

The Kingdom of God works through relationship, revelation, and through resignation. This will answer your question, "How come I never hear a *rhema* word directly to me? God, I'll do anything." I hear the Holy Spirit saying, "Really?" You see, we must resign from being in control of our lives and surrender to His lordship and authority. God will test you. God writes down when you say yes and He writes down when you say no. Do you want great faith? You have to be faithful in little faith. Before you obey Him in the great and miraculous, obey Him in the little. How can you whip cancer when you are always taking an aspirin for your headache?

We must totally surrender to His rulership. This is true submission and obedience. I'm talking about unmitigated, undiluted submission and obedience to God. It will never go against the word of God; that's your guideline.

We must allow the Holy Spirit to transform and renew our thinking to a Kingdom mindset. **Romans 12:1** – "I beseech you therefore, brethren, by the mercies of God, that you present your bodies a living sacrifice, holy, acceptable to God, which is your reasonable service. Do not be conformed to this world, but be transformed by the renewing of your mind," or your thinking.

You need to go from impossibility thinking to possibility thinking. You need to go from "I'm in control" thinking to "God's in control" thinking.

Submission and obedience are voluntary; but if we fail to practice them, we will live contrary to God's Kingdom and rebellion will operate in our hearts. Can you be a Christian and rebellious? I'd like to think in His grace yes, but you will forfeit moving in the Kingdom *rhema* from God.

Life Lesson: Being under authority is the key to exercising authority.

Romans 13:1-2 says to be subject to every authority. For every authority that's on earth has been ordained by God and whoever resists the authority resists God. If the sign says 55 mph, you drive 54 mph. If you can't listen to a man's sign that says, "Keep off the grass," how are you going to command a demon to get out.

This especially applies to all students: stop answering back to your parents. Obey the curfew. Stop asking them, "Well, when you were my age what time did you get home?" First of all, when they were your age, they didn't have cell phones. They didn't have texting and sexting and all that other stuff. Secondly, your father and mother remember what they did; that's why they're scared! If you can't submit to them, whom you've seen, how are you going to submit to God, whom you've not seen?

The Kingdom of Satan

Let's look at how the Kingdom of Satan works.

How does the Kingdom of Satan rule? Number one, he rules through darkness. He loves darkness.

Darkness

2 Corinthians 4:3-4 reads: "But even if our gospel is veiled, it is veiled to those who are perishing, whose minds the god of this age has blinded, who do not believe, lest the light of the gospel of the glory of Christ who is the image of God, should shine on them." Satan loves darkness. I'm talking about spiritual darkness. You can talk to some people until you're blue and it's just like water off a duck's back.

Break the blindness before you preach the gospel. Come against the blindness. Turn the light on. Speak **Ephesians 1:17-19** over them. I speak about Mary; I speak about John. I declare that the light of the Word of God, the eyes of his understanding would be made open that when I speak to them the bell is going to go off, the elevator is going to the last floor, and he's going to understand and he'll have to fight not to get saved. You need to pray before you preach. Amen? The whole world is like that.

Ephesians 5:8-11 "For you were once in darkness," listen when we preach to people, please remember that you once were messed up and unsaved. "You were once in darkness but now you are light in the Lord. Walk as children of light (for the fruit of the Spirit is in all goodness, righteousness, and truth), finding out what is acceptable to the Lord."

Before you witness to people, make sure you are walking right. Don't tell them about the light of the gospel when you are a rebel. When you're in a restaurant ordering a beer and a drink. Ok? You say, "Well, there's nothing wrong with a beer or an alcoholic drink." There's a lot of alcoholics over here who are desperately trying to end alcohol and when they see you in there ordering that, they'll fall right off the wagon and you would have pushed them there. Don't preach the light if you are going to be grey. Don't preach the light unless you are wearing sunglasses.

The Kingdom of Satan subjugates; that means

imprisons. It subjects by keeping them unaware of or blinded to their lost spiritual condition, their purpose on earth, and the power of Jesus Christ through the cross and resurrection. You live near people; you may go to school with people, and you may work with people. We have a great opportunity to walk in the light of Jesus. **Ephesians 5:7** So we need to "become blameless and harmless children of God without fault, in the midst of a crooked and perverse generation, among whom you shine as lights in the world. **Philippians 2:15**

Disobedience

Satan rules through disobedience. He absolutely loves disobedience. **Ephesians 2:2-3** says: "In which you once walked according to the course of this world, according to the prince of the power of the air, the spirit who now works in the sons of disobedience, among whom also we all once conducted ourselves in the lusts of the flesh, fulfilling the desires of the flesh and of the mind, and were by nature children of wrath, just as the others."

Satan loves disobedience. He loves when people think, "I don't see anything wrong with that." Well, who are you? "I just don't see anything wrong with that." Die to yourself. If you died to yourself, maybe you will understand what the Bible says. When the Bible says don't do it, it's not a suggestion. It means the ten commandments are not ten suggestions. Disobedience is either voluntary or the result of spiritual ignorance. Honestly, there were some things I was just rebellious as could be. Other things, I never knew.

I never knew that the Bible spoke against that. I remember I used to pray to spirits; I thought it was God until I read **Deuteronomy 18:9-14** and I got so convicted.

I said, "God, I'm going to hell. I'm talking to demons." I didn't know that. Did you know that many people who live near you on your block, who go to high school and college with you, are in ignorance? Either they're blind or they're in ignorance. Be careful with them! Be loving with them. Be gentle with them. Reveal light little by little. Have you ever been in the dark and you come into the sunlight and you cover your eyes? Why? Your pupils were open and now they have to adjust. When somebody's in darkness, give them the light little-by-little.

These individuals do not realize that Satan controls them. They don't realize that. They think they're in control of their lives. They're not in control; if Jesus is not in control then the devil is in control. **Ephesians 2:2-3** Perhaps there is such a thing as a carnal Christian. In **1 Corinthians 3:3** we read about being carnal. The problem is in **Romans 8:6**, it says to be carnally minded is death. You can't stay carnal for a long time. Therefore, I want to tell you this: many people who attend churches in Canada, the United Kingdom, and the United States, they claim to be born again, but they are not born again. They've been deceived because they have been in control. They always have been in control, and they intend to stay in control of their own lives and destinies. Are you one of them? Are you in control of your life?

Many think they're born again, but they retain control of their lives. You need to give Him full control.

Domination

We who are aware and are a part of God's Kingdom must intercede and intervene to set them free. Intercede before you intervene. Intervene means you go into their space, you talk to them and say, "Listen, you can't keep doing that." In other words, pray before you preach. Satan exercises and rules through darkness, disobedience, and through domination. Before Christ I was involved in witchcraft; I didn't realize it, but I was. More importantly than that, I ruled my own life. I'll not quote **Ephesians 2:1-3** again but domination is a spirit of control.

First of all, to dominate means when Satan makes people do what he wants to through intimidation, witchcraft, or controlling individuals. Satan loves to manipulate and intimidate so that he can dominate. He would love to use you to do it. When I was a young Christian, God gave me a revealed word that I never forgot. I was reading about the works of the flesh and the fruit of the Spirit and He told me this, "I want you to do all the fruit of the Spirit." I said, "I got it! I got it! I'll do it! I'll do it!" And He said, "And look at yourself as capable of doing any of the works of the flesh." I realized that as I see my potential to do the works of the flesh, I can overcome them by the fruit of the Spirit.

Galatians 5:19-21 reads: adultery, fornication, outbursts of wrath, drunkenness, then you get to verse 20, witchcraft. What? Many people would say, "I've never done or had anything to do with witchcraft." The word is *pharmakia*. Witchcraft basically is the spirit of control. It's natural to us; if you don't believe me, when it's Christmas season, go to a mall and watch the little boy walk past a toy store and have a hissy fit when mom says, "We can't afford that." He screams and pouts. "Ok! I'll get it!" "Thank you Mama!" Instant deliverance. I used to hear my kids whisper to each other. Carissa would tell David, "David, if you want that, you ask Dad. He always says yes. But if you want that, you ask mom, dad will always say no." They had us pegged. They were natural manipulators; they were born that way.

We like to have our way. We do! We enjoy it! To dominate means Satan makes people do what he wants them to do through intimidation or witchcraft. This is a work of the flesh or a demon. Warning: beware that you do not intentionally or inadvertently exercise control over others either by crafty manipulation or by fearful intimidation. I am good at certain things. All of us who are good at certain things, especially if you are in business and you are used to making the final decision; and be careful that you don't always insist on being right and having your way. You're a business man and you come home and your wife says, "I want to..." "No! I don't see it that way!" "Well, honey can't we...?" "No, woman, submit!" Be careful when you're very good at something, that you don't step on other people. You might mean well but you could be intimidating them or manipulating them. Warning: is there any sin such as unforgiveness, outbursts of wrath, drug abuse, drunkenness, lust, pornography that is dominating and controlling you? If the answer is yes; there is probably demonic oppression in your life. If you've been trying to kick something and it keeps biting you, call and make an appointment to see a Spirit-led pastor. You may need prayer for deliverance.

Life Lesson: Don't let anything master you but the Master.

Life Lesson: A person with a controlling spirit must always have their own way in their dealings with others.

Do you always have to be right? Do you always have to have your own way? Be careful! If you are displeased when you don't always get your way, it could be a rising spirit of control and that is from Satan, not God.

CHAPTER FIVE

How To Apply Jesus' Victory In Your Life

"Having disarmed principalities and powers, He made a public spectacle of them, triumphing over them in it." **Colossians 2:15**

"When a strong man, fully armed, guards his own palace, his goods are in peace. But when a stronger than he comes upon him and overcomes him, he takes from him all his armor in which he trusted, and divides his spoils." **Luke 11:21-22**

"Inasmuch then as the children have partaken of flesh and blood, He Himself likewise shared in the same, that through death He might destroy him who had the power of death, that is, the devil," **Hebrews 2:14**

"In which you once walked according to the course of this world, according to the prince of the power of the air, the spirit who now works in the sons of disobedience," **Ephesians 2:2**

"That the God of our Lord Jesus Christ, the Father of glory, may give to you the spirit of wisdom and revelation in the knowledge of Him, the eyes of your understanding being enlightened; that you may know what is the hope of His calling, what are the riches of the glory of His inheritance in the saints, and what is the exceeding greatness of His power toward us who believe, according to the working of His mighty power which He worked in Christ when He raised Him from the dead and seated Him at His right hand in the Heavenly places, far above all principality and power and might and dominion, and every name that is named, not only in this age but also in that which is to come. And He put all things under His feet, and gave Him to be head over all things to the church, which is His body, the fullness of Him who fills all in all." **Ephesians 1:17-23**

Key Take Away: At the cross and by the resurrection, Jesus secured victory over Satan and his allies in the air but each of us must now apply that victory.

A quick review: The Kingdom of God is the government of God. The Kingdom of God means the rulership of God. Jesus came preaching the gospel of the Kingdom. I thank God for the cross and the blood and the resurrection, but that gets you into the Kingdom. The Kingdom of God is a whole lot more. It's God totally controlling you and then flowing through you to bring Heaven on earth right here, right now.

Every country, every city has invisible fallen angels over it, but you know what, we're not concerned about them because Jesus whipped them and now we have to take that victory and we have to apply it.

Satan has been initially defeated. I want you to see that Jesus conquered Satan at the cross. This is so critically important; we are going to take time with this right now. You see, Satan has been initially defeated. Well, what do you mean by initially? The work of the cross was an inauguration. It was only the beginning; where Jesus fully defeated Satan, where every demon in hell, where every power and principality did everything they could to stop Jesus from shedding His blood and purchasing our salvation. It was an initial victory in this sense.

Please understand one day with the Lord is as 1,000 years. God's not in a hurry. When Jesus defeats Satan at the cross, his defeat was in phases. In Revelation 20, we find that Satan is finally tied up in chains and then thrown into the Lake of Fire. But what exactly happened at the cross where He initially defeated him?

Let's read **Colossians 2:15** in the Amplified and it says, "[God] disarmed the principalities and powers that were ranged against us and made a bold display and public example of them, in triumphing over them in Him and in it [the cross]."

I want you to know three keywords here: bold display, public example, and triumphing. The word triumphing is a military term. It's a Roman military term. When a Roman general went off to war and he was victorious, it was understood that the territories that he conquered were now going to be part of the Kingdom of Rome. When he came back they gave him beautiful white horses and a gorgeous chariot; he wore resplendent armor and the people would hold what we would call a parade. Both sides of the street, they would be whooping and hollering, cheering because Rome has gotten bigger and the enemy is defeated.

Bold display means that all of the captured generals, the captured officers, and the men were chained to the chariot and they would follow the chariot and the people would cheer and all of the spoils, the gold and material from that country, were displayed in the streets of Rome. But I'm here to tell you a story. When Jesus Christ, died, the devil thought he had a victory. The devil thought, "I finally got rid of Jesus." Then the Bible says, that He descended into the inner part of the earth, into sheol, into hell and he thought Jesus was dead. He had the devil, I'm speaking metaphorically right now, He had him line up and chained up and He said, "Satan, you had the keys to hell and death. I have the keys to life. But you know what? I want you to hand over your keys. You no longer have the keys of hell and death! You no longer have uninterrupted, unobscured, unopposed power to send people to hell! Give me those keys right now! Give me the keys right now!"

We read in **Matthew 16:18-19** when He told Peter, "And I also say to you that you are Peter and on this rock I will build my church and the gates of hell shall not prevail against it." Then He goes on to say, "And I will give you, church, the keys of the Kingdom of Heaven." Whatever you loose on earth, will be loosed in Heaven.

A key is an instrument that gives you access to something that was locked. I have a key to my car; it gives me access to my car. Jesus said, "I'm giving you the keys to the Kingdom of Heaven. All that Heaven has to offer, all the salvation, the healing, the prosperity, all that Heaven has to offer I give it to you. I'm handing it to you and whatever you unlock on earth, I'll unlock it in Heaven and whatever you bind on earth, I'll bind it in Heaven."

We read in **Revelation 1:18** "I am He who lives, and was dead, and behold, I am alive forevermore. I have the keys of Hades and of Death." I lined Satan up and I told him, "Let me have those keys, let me have all your trophies, let me see all your generals. They mean nothing because I take my blood, place it on the tabernacle in Heaven, on the mercy seat and My blood sets them free!" Glory to God! Devil, give me your keys. You no longer have unopposed power; you know what?

I have the keys now and you can't send people to hell unless they want to go there. He gives the Church those keys. You've got a key in your hand; make sure you use it.

Satan was initially defeated.

Satan Has Been Initially Dethroned

But secondly, Satan has been initially dethroned. Now, you understand the true meaning of **Luke 11:21-22** when He says, "When a strong man, fully armed, guards his own palace, his goods are in peace. But when a stronger than he comes upon him and overcomes him, he takes from him all his armor in which he trusted, and divides his spoils."

Do you know what Jesus was talking about? This is Kingdom language! The strong man represents Satan, represents the devil, and Jesus was kind of broadcasting to the whole world that this time, even to the devil, "Devil, you know what I'm about to do and you can't stop me." The stronger man represents Jesus. If the strong man represents Satan, the stronger man represents Jesus then what's the palace? The palace, "He guards his own palace," represents the Kingdom of the earth that Satan rules, ruled at that time unopposed. He can do what he wants, had everybody; anybody that died probably went to hell at that time. Not all the world had heard the law of God.

What does fully armed mean? Fully armed, guards his own palace, his goods are in peace. It means Satan felt secure in his army of demons in maintaining control over people; people are the goods on the earth.

Jesus, the stronger man, defeated Satan, removed

him from his throne, removed him from his rulership, and stripped him of his authority and power. His authority and power is that he had the keys of hell and death but no longer was humanity to fear dying because now we can guarantee that we can go to the Kingdom of Heaven.

Guillermo Maldonado says, "When Jesus was victorious over the enemy, He divided the spoils of His triumph with humanity and gave dominion of the earth back to you and I."[25] We are the ones that have dominion now. Now we can fulfill the prayer – our Father who art in Heaven, hallowed be Thy name. Thy Kingdom come, thy will be done on earth...I said on earth...as it is in Heaven. We bring the Kingdom of God here on earth. We displace the devil here on earth in the power of Heaven. From now on every Christian, here it is, has the potential to dethrone Satan from their hearts and from their lives.

A great evangelical man named S.D. Gordon said, "In every heart there is a cross and a throne, and each is occupied. If Jesus is on the throne, ruling self is on the cross, dying. But if self is being obeyed, and so is ruling, then it is on the throne and self on the throne means that Jesus has been put on the cross."[26] You can believe in knowledge of Jesus. You can dethrone Satan from you heart. In my ministry, I have experienced much pain and suffering. I understand the grief, but greater is the victory that He obtained for you than the grief you suffered. You're not alone anymore. I know your husband is gone, but you know who your husband now? Jesus Christ, the King of kings and the Lord of lords.

I want to address you now if you are a married

couple. You can dethrone Satan from your home. You can kick out strife and contention, no longer confess, "Well, I don't love my wife" or "I don't love my husband." Make a decision to love her right now and to love him right now in the name of Jesus and stop bellyaching. She's changed, so have you bubba. You've changed, too. We need to make a decision not to mention the word "divorce" anymore. Mention the word dethroned and no longer divorce. I want to speak to all my students. You dethrone the devil from your heart. You don't let your friends dictate what you are going to do. Remember, the voices you hear determine the choices you make. Who you hang out with is going to determine your destiny. Listen: dethrone the devil from your heart, live for God, keep your virginity, preach Jesus, and live in victory!

Satan has been Initially Disarmed

Satan has been initially disarmed. I wanted to be sure to write the best that I can. I called Dr. Zach Tackett from Southeastern University, a Biblical scholar, just to run my conclusions by him. I have always been troubled by what I'm going to share with you. **Colossians 2:15**, the English Standard Version, "He (Jesus) disarmed the rulers and authorities and put them to open shame, by triumphing over them in him." How can you explain **Ephesians 6:12**? I know the Bible doesn't contradict itself but it says, "For we do not wrestle against flesh and blood, but against principalities, against powers, against the rulers of the darkness of this age, against spiritual hosts of wickedness in the Heavenly places."

Wait a minute! Didn't He disarm them? If He disarmed them, why do we wrestle against them? The Lord revealed it to me. Does **Colossians 2:15** contradict **Ephesians 6:12**? No, it doesn't contradict **Ephesians**

6:12. Not when you understand that the victory over the devil was in phases. It was his inaugural defeat. When Jesus beat Satan, He defeated him from stopping Jesus from going to the cross, taking His blood, and putting it on the mercy seat. There was nothing the devil could do about it, but now it's up to you and me to take that victory and apply it every day of our lives. The cross and the resurrection disarms Satan's rulers and authorities in the Heavenlies and prevented them. There was nothing the devil, the demons, and the principalities can do at that moment with Jesus.

The Church has the potential to execute this authority over the same rulers, over the same authorities to set people free in the name of Jesus. Now it's our turn, as the Church, to fully understand that He's put the principalities, the powers of darkness under our feet. Now we've got to live that out. When I go to another country, I don't concern myself about binding the powers of the air, I just go and preach Jesus. I just go and cast out demons and declare the Kingdom of God. I'm not worried about what's in the Heavenlies. I'm concerned about executing the Kingdom of God right here on earth and people get saved and they get set free and it can happen with you as well. Now you understand why both scriptures don't contradict each other because the first scripture dealt with Jesus' victory, the second scripture talks about our everyday life and we have to apply that victory.

Ephesians 3:10-12 says, so that through the church, through who? Through the church, "The manifold wisdom of God might be made known..." known to who? Look, you're known to who? The rulers and authorities in Heavenly places. You know why you're known? Because they can't touch you. This was, "According to the eternal purpose which He accomplished in Christ Jesus our Lord, in whom we have boldness and access with confidence through faith in Him." Jesus not only was the leader, Jesus raises leaders. We're not only saved by the blood of Jesus, now we take ownership and rulership over those same powers and principalities, preach Jesus, get people set free, and there's not a thing they can do against you when you realize that you are a son/daughter of the King of kings and the Lord of lords over the whole universe.

Now you understand **Ephesians 3:14-20** "For this reason I bow my knees to the Father of our Lord Jesus Christ, from whom the whole family in Heaven and earth is named, that He would grant you, according to the riches of His glory, to be strengthened with might through His Spirit in the inner man, that Christ may dwell in your hearts through faith; that you, being rooted and grounded in love, may be able to comprehend with all the saints what is the width and length and depth and height – to know the love of Christ which passes knowledge; that you may be filled with all the fullness of God."

Fullness means this, you take the victory on the cross and bring it down here right now. "Now to Him who is able to do exceedingly abundantly above all that we ask or think, according to the power that works in us." **Ephesians 3:20** That power is faith. If you believe that that same victory was purchased, if you believe that in My Name you shall cast out demons, that in My Name you shall lay hands on the sick and they will recover. If you believe that greater works than these you shall do, you shall have what you say!

Every Christian can now appropriate authority over

Satan and his rulers and authorities to walk in personal victory and deliver captives from the Kingdom of Satan.

Prior to Jesus' victory, Satan and his rulers and authorities controlled whole countries and the world's populations. There was nothing that kings and rulers and governors could do. That's why people cried in a funeral; they wept. "We'll never see them again." There was no hope of any resurrection. But we serve a God who took the keys of hell and death and now we can see our loved ones again. We're going to live forever. Hallelujah!

There's an option. Before Jesus' victory there was no option. If you left this world, you went to Sheol (located in the middle of the earth) **Luke 16:19-31**. But now there's an option. In Jesus' name we can have the victory and this is a struggle that we as Christians wrestle against. You see before there was no struggle, we were bound by Satan. There's a struggle now because one part of us wants to serve God, and there is another part of us that wants to serve you. Do you know about that inner struggle?

Romans 8:23 says this, "Not only that, but we also who have the firstfruits of the Spirit, even we ourselves groan within ourselves, eagerly awaiting for the adoption, the redemption of our body." You know what that means? As long as we are in this mortal body there is going to be a fight. That's why **Galatians 5:16** says, "Walk in the Spirit, and you shall not fulfill the lust of the flesh." But if you fulfill the lust of the flesh then you can't walk in the Spirit. That fight's going to be over when the trumpet is going to sound and we're all going to be taken up. That day, that fight's going to be over. If you just happen to die, immediately, to be absent from the body is to be present with the Lord.

In the meantime, there's going to be groaning. There's going to be, "Ah! I can't believe I said that!" "I can't believe I did that! I can't believe I was thinking about that!" That's the struggle that we're going to have and every day we execute...that's why Jesus said in Luke 9:23 we carry our cross daily. Daily, we have to carry it.

Satan's unlimited power has been destroyed. His unlimited power of what? Of casting people into hell, of bringing the fear of death. Jesus came to destroy the works of Satan. **1 John 3:8b** says, "For this purpose the Son of God was manifested, that He might destroy the works of the devil." He's still destroying the works of the evil one every time you get somebody saved, every time you get somebody healed, every time you get somebody delivered, every time you make a disciple. You're still destroying the works of Satan.

Jesus' death and resurrection broke the power of Satan to send people to hell after death, to bind people with continuous sin, sickness, and poverty. There is no reason why you have to continually be bound by any sin, by any demon. There is deliverance in Jesus. Can you believe that? Before the keys were taken from the devil there was no option; now there is. I want to ask you something: will you now take that option and be completely free from every sin, from every carnality? We need to do that, my friend.

The Church now has the authority to enforce Christ's victory, to keep on destroying the works of Satan by delivering people through supernatural revelation and manifestation. Hey, you can't argue with a miracle. We are people who bring miracles. We need high school students who are bold to go into the schools and lay hands on the sick right there in the hallway. We need widows, housewives, married couples who are going to take it to Walmart. Right there in Walmart, lay hands on the sick and they'll recover. You might be saying, "Pastor, I've never heard anything like this before." It's happening in the U.S. and around the world so come get in on the action! Don't stay behind!

We need to understand that Satan is still dangerous. I know that there are a lot of people that say an old lion roars because he has no teeth. This is a fact, but lions also kill by breaking the spine of their prey with their limbs.[27]

When Peter says, through the Holy Spirit, be sober. **1 Peter 5:8-9** "Be sober, be vigilant; because your adversary the devil walks about like a roaring lion, seeking whom he may devour." Who do you think killed those people in Iraq when they got beheaded? That was the devil inspiring them. If the devil was completely and totally defeated, those babies would still be alive. There is evil out there. When you see the worst murders, that's the devil! He's still walking around.

It was Satan who used the terrorist Omar Marteen to slaughter 49 people and wound 53 others at the Pulse Night Club in Orlando, Florida on June 12, 2016. It was Satan who inspired Mohamed Lahouaiej-Bouhel to drive a rented truck into a crowd in Nice, France, killing 84 people on July 16, 2016. He still wants to destroy you. Verse 9 is for you, "Resist him, steadfast in the faith, knowing that the same sufferings are experienced by your brotherhood in the world."

Satan's final defeat will be in the book of Revelation. By the way, the devil knows the Bible inside and out so he knows his days are limited. He knows **Revelation 20:10**, "The devil, who deceived them, was cast into the lake of fire and brimstone where the beast [the antichrist] and the false prophet are. And they will be tormented day and night forever and ever." I remember telling a Satanist, "You want to serve Lucifer and Satan. I want you to know he's going to bake in the lake. He does not rule in hell. He burns and screams there." Do you understand what I'm saying? The devil knows he's going to scream and burn forever; he just wants you to join him. He wants your mother to join him. He wants your husband/wife to join him. He wants your best friends in school to join him. Don't let them join him. Open up your mouth tomorrow morning and tell them about Jesus before they go to hell!

Never use the expression, "Go to hell!" You are cursing somebody into an eternity of flames.

Satan retains three legal rights to fight against the true Christians:

Number one, temptation. **James 1:14-15** "But each one is tempted when he is drawn away by his own desires and enticed." Take ownership over your desires. "Then, when desire has conceived it gives birth to sin; and sin, when it is full grown, brings forth death." I want you to see this Bible pattern on how the devil deceives us. First of all, it begins with deception. The devil is a liar; he twists everything. Let me just quote two scriptures to you. **James 1:22**, "But be doers of the word, and not hearers only, deceiving yourselves." Do you know how you deceive yourself? Let's say it says, "You need to forgive." "Oh, I'm not that type of person. I don't forgive easily." You just deceived yourself. You didn't even need the devil to deceive you; you just talked yourself out of obeying God. "I can't give this habit up."

You just deceived yourself. I thought the Bible says I can do all things through Christ who strengthens me. You just fooled yourself. Why would God command you to do something and then not give you the strength, power, and grace in order to do it? Don't deceive yourself anymore by saying, "I'm not that type of person. I was not born that way." You need to check yourself out.

Then I want to warn everybody about **Deuteronomy 29:14-19**, I call this strange peace which I mentioned earlier. You watch out for strange peace. What does that mean? You watch out for saying something… "You know I prayed about it and I feel good about it." Even though you know it is sin.

Deuteronomy 29, beginning in verse 14, this is Moses with the nation of Israel, "I make this covenant and this oath, not with you alone, but with him who stands here with us today before the Lord our God, as well as with him who is not here with us today [that means us] (for you know that we dwelt in the land of Egypt and that we came through the nations which you passed by, and you saw their abominations and their idols which were among them – wood and stone and silver and gold); so that there may not be among you man or woman or family or tribe, whose heart turns away today from the Lord our God, to go and serve the gods of these nations, and that there may not be among you a root bearing bitterness or wormwood; and so it may not happen, when he hears the words of this curse, that he blesses himself in his heart, saying, 'I shall have peace, even though I follow the dictates of my heart' – as though the drunkard could be included with the sober."

Next time somebody is living with somebody, taking crack cocaine or meth and they tell you, "You know, I still love Jesus. I have a peace." They have just blessed themselves, they have strange peace, and they will split hell wide open, my friend. When the Word of God tells you something or your authority who loves you, it behooves you to do something. Don't come back to us and say, "Well, I prayed about it and I feel good about it." We prayed about it too and you're wrong. It's easier to argue with the human flesh than to argue with God. It sounds like this, "Well, I don't see it that way."

Literally, I met a young man recently who told me, "I'm living with my girlfriend. We are trying it out to see if we are compatible with each other." I said, "Fornicators will not inherit the Kingdom of God. **Hebrews 13:4** says: "Let the bed be undefiled and whoremongers will not inherit the Kingdom of God." And he told me, "Well, I don't see it that way. I feel real good about it." He had strange peace. But my girlfriend feels good about it too and my parents. What do they know? What do your parents know?

What does the Word of God say? It begins with deception. Deception will give you desires. Desires that are ungodly, desires that are unscriptural, desires for another man's wife. "Well, I don't love my wife anymore. You know, we're just incompatible." Too bad, so sad. You make yourself love her by faith and with the Grace of God. You made a covenant at the altar. You said, "I do," and now you won't. Well, I've been told this. "We're going to divorce our spouse, get married, and repent afterwards."

Romans 6:1 says shall we sin that grace may abound? God forbid! There is no salvation for pre-meditated sin. That's not repentance, my friend. We need to stop that. Desire turns into disobedience when you finally go against the Word of God. What was Israel's disobedience?

There's two things that lead to strange peace: idolatry, which is the exalting of a person, place, or thing above God, and bitterness. Don't you allow idolatry and bitterness...don't you make an idol of your family. "I would come to Christ, but you know my family is Catholic and they would be upset." That's why you don't come to Christ? Jesus taught that we should not love family more than Him. **Luke 14:26-33** They're like me. I grew up a Catholic, but when I saw the light, I left that. But praise God that God in His mercy is saving many Catholics in these last days!

Disobedience leads to destruction. No worse destruction than the day that you breathe your last and you wake up in flames of hell, my friend. I don't know about you, but I can smell those flames right now. Hell is calling your name!

Jesus preached more on hell than He did love and you need to understand I love the love of God, but I also love the fear of God. Then the devil uses persecution. If you get on fire for God, you're going to get repercussions. I want to serve God and let the persecutions come. Who are you bothering today? If you're not bothering somebody, maybe you're a part of the crowd.

Secondly, Satan uses persecution. **Matthew 5:11-12** reads: "Blessed are you when they revile and persecute you, and say all kinds of evil against you falsely for My sake. Rejoice and be exceedingly glad, for great is your reward in Heaven, for so they persecuted the prophets who were before you." Don't go to prayer meeting and say, "Please pray for me, nobody likes me." They're not supposed to like you. With Jesus, you either loved Him or hated Him. People will hate the Jesus in you.

2 Corinthians 2:14-16 says we let out an aroma. To the unsaved we smell like perdition, to the saved we smell great. No deodorant can put out that smell. But if they don't smell Jesus, I invite you to give your life to Jesus. **Philippians 1:29** "For to you it has been granted on behalf of Christ, not only to believe in Him, but also to suffer for His sake."

Are you suffering for Jesus? Is somebody not liking you? Is somebody talking about you? Is somebody saying false things against you? If they are, that's normal! Be nervous if nobody's talking about you. Be nervous if in the factory people say, "I've known you for 20 years and I didn't know you were a Christian." "Wow! You're a Christian? You could have fooled me!" Since you walk like everybody else, you talk like everybody else. You see friends the enemy will attack anyone who dares to carry out God's will. That's why a lot of Christians don't witness because we don't want to be talked about.

He will try to destroy anyone who wants to establish the Kingdom bringing the rulership of God down here. He will attack and oppose people who want to set people free from demonic bondage, sickness or sin. They usually say this to you, "You're a fanatic. They can go to a psychiatrist; they need pills and medication." You don't sedate demons. You can't tranquilize the devil.

He is not willing to surrender the territory he has gained, and people are territories, and will attack with all wickedness and power when he feels threatened. He will give you temptation. He will give you persecution and thirdly, Satan will use accusation. **Revelation 12:10** "Then I heard a loud voice saying in Heaven, 'Now salvation, and strength, and the Kingdom of our God, and the power of His Christ have come, for the accuser of our brethren, who accused them before our God day and night, has been cast down." What does Satan accuse you of?

He will accuse you of sin to bring guilt. He wants you to feel bad about something you've repented about 200 times. Then he'll bring it again and he'll say things like this, "The reason you remember is because you are not forgiven. You haven't changed a bit." Have you heard that voice before? Somebody once said, "When the devil brings up your past, you bring up his future." You tell him he's going to bake in the lake! He has no fear of God; therefore, he has no wisdom.

Satan uses people, especially fleshly Christians, to bring accusations which cause strife and offense. I hate to say it, but people come every Sunday to church and they are full of the flesh. Jesus even said in the parable of the wheat and the tares, only until the end will I reveal who really was a servant of the devil and who really was a servant of God. He will use Christians, or in name Christians, to accuse you; always bringing up your past, you know this happened to me today. Somebody came to me about somebody in the church, "Did you know…did you know?" I said, "Yeah, that's the way they were."

Get this in your spirit: There is an epidemic of people being easily offended. Easily offended is one of the great signs that Jesus is coming soon. **Matthew 24:10** "And then many," what does the Greek word many mean?

A whole lot of people. "Then many will be offended, will betray one another." People are being offended over the stupidest things. You're sitting in my seat. The pastor walked by me and didn't smile. Forgive him for being human! You didn't bury a 5-year-old yesterday; he did. You didn't look at a little 5-year-old boy in a casket; he did. Maybe he's got a burden in his heart. Stop being offended in Jesus' name and if you are offended, forgive them right away. You need to look at them and say, "That's why Jesus died because she's so irritable. Hallelujah! I forgive her in Jesus' name." I didn't say you shouldn't avoid them when they come up to you. I'm just saying stop being offended! Many are offended because they are busybodies into what others are doing wrong because they have a wrong spirit. I feel a word of the Lord. We need divine wisdom on how to treat people. Many are so easily offended. We need to watch our response, the way we respond. We need to think for a moment before we snap into judgment.

The Holy Spirit is dealing with us. If people are so easily offended, maybe they are not offended with something you did but with another. But I want to warn you, some people wake up offended. People are sometimes tools of accusation. Please say, "Holy Spirit speak to me." People who are tools of accusation are generally unforgiving, negative, complaining, and faultfinding. If the devil wants you to be his puppet in accusing somebody it means that you have an unforgiving nature, you're very negative. The sun could be out and you would say, "Yep, but it's going to rain," always complaining, always finding fault. Am I guilty of accusation?

CHAPTER SIX

Kingdom-Minded Christians Impact Others

"Then He lifted up His eyes toward His disciples, and said: "Blessed **are you poor, For yours is the Kingdom of God. Blessed are you** who hunger now, For you shall be filled. Blessed **are you** who weep now, For you shall laugh. Blessed are you when men hate you, And when they exclude you, And **revile** you, and cast out your name as evil, For the Son of Man's sake. Rejoice in that day and leap for joy! For indeed your reward **is** great in Heaven, For in like manner their fathers did to the prophets. "But woe to you who are rich, For you have received your consolation. Woe to you who are full, For you shall hunger. Woe to you who laugh now, For you shall mourn and weep. Woe to you when all men speak well of you, For so did their fathers to the false prophets. "But I say to you who hear: Love your enemies, do good to those who hate you, bless those who curse you, and pray for those who spitefully use you. To him who strikes you on the **one** cheek, offer the other also. And from him who takes away **your** cloak, do not withhold your tunic either. Give to everyone who asks of you. And from him who takes away your goods do not ask **them** back. And just as you want men to do to you, you also do to them likewise. "But if you love those who love you, what credit is that to you? For even sinners love those who love them. And if you do good to those who do good to you, what credit is that to you?

For even sinners do the same. And if you lend **to those** from whom you hope to receive back, what credit is that to you? For even sinners lend to sinners to receive as much back. But love your enemies, do good, and lend, hoping for nothing in return; and your reward will be great, and you will be sons of the Most High. For He is kind to the unthankful and evil. Therefore be merciful, just as your Father also is merciful. "Judge not, and you shall not be judged. Condemn not, and you shall not be condemned. Forgive, and you will be forgiven. Give, and it will be given to you: good measure, pressed down, shaken together, and running over will be put into your bosom. For with the same measure that you use, it will be measured back to you." And He spoke a parable to them: "Can the blind lead the blind? Will they not both fall into the ditch? A disciple is not above his teacher, but everyone who is perfectly trained will be like his teacher. And why do you look at the speck in your brother's eye, but do not perceive the plank in your own eye? Or how can you say to your brother, 'Brother, let me remove the speck that is in your eye,' when you yourself do not see the plank that is in your own eye? Hypocrite! First remove the plank from your own eye, and then you will see clearly to remove the speck that is in your brother's eye. "For a good tree does not bear bad fruit, nor does a bad tree bear good fruit. For every tree is known by its own fruit. For **men** do not gather figs from thorns, nor do they gather grapes from a bramble bush. A good man out of the good treasure of his heart brings forth good; and an evil man out of the evil treasure of his heart brings forth evil. For out of the abundance of the heart his mouth speaks. "But why do you call Me 'Lord, Lord,' and not do the things which I say? Whoever comes to Me, and hears My sayings and does them, I will show you whom he is like: He is like a man building a house, who dug deep and laid the foundation on the rock. And when the flood arose, the stream beat vehemently against that house, and could not shake it, for it was founded on the rock. But he who heard and did nothing is like a man who built a house on the earth without a foundation, against which the stream beat vehemently; and immediately it fell. And the ruin of that house was great." **Luke 6:20-49**

Key Take Away: Kingdom-minded Christians impact others with their attitude, actions, speech, and love.

Kingdom people have a different culture all together. In America, we have different cultures. You have the biker culture; you have Indian culture. You have different types of groups, hundreds, but in the Kingdom culture, we all have something in common. We have the same King (Jesus) and the same Heavenly Father. We have the same mission: to impact others with the way we live.

I want to read **1 Thessalonians 2:11-12** from the English Standard Version: "For you know how, like a father with his children, we exhorted each one of you and encouraged you and charged you to walk in a manner worthy of God, who calls you into his own Kingdom and glory."

The key take away is so important for YOU! There

is something I want you to take with you for the rest of your life: Kingdom-minded Christians impact others with their attitude, actions, speech, and love.

Unusual Beatitudes

We're going to break down what's often called the Sermon on the Mount. First of all, let's go to unusual beatitudes. Someone correctly said the beatitudes simply are the attitudes you ought to be and Kingdom minded people have these attitudes.

Luke 6:20-23 reads: "Then He lifted up His eyes toward His disciples, and said: 'Blessed **are you** poor, for yours is the Kingdom of God. Blessed **are you** who hunger now, for you shall be filled. Blessed **are you** who weep now, for you shall laugh. Blessed are you when men hate you, and when they exclude you, and revile **you**, and cast out your name as evil, for the Son of Man's sake. Rejoice in that day and leap for joy! For indeed your reward is great in Heaven, for in like manner their fathers did to the prophets.'"

The Blessing of Being Disadvantaged

What kind of attitude is this? I want you to envision thousands of people on this mountain; the disciples are there, people are just cramming, and His voice projects over and you begin to hear Jesus say these things. He first speaks of the blessing of being disadvantaged. Disadvantaged of what? It says blessed are the poor. He is not talking about material poor. He's not talking about not having any money. He's talking about being poor in your spirit. He's talking about that you're so desperate in your need for God that you can't make it in life without Him. That's how poor you feel. He's talking about that you are so bankrupt of righteousness that you need God just to have any ounce of goodness.

The Blessing of Being Dissatisfied

He continues and He talks about the blessing of being dissatisfied and people are just hanging on His words when He says in **Luke 6:21**, "Blessed are you who hunger now, for you shall be filled." Dissatisfied with one's spiritual condition. You're dissatisfied with your spiritual poverty. You're dissatisfied that you need everything that God has. That you don't have any ounce of goodness in you or righteousness outside of God and you hunger for God to fill you.

The Blessing of Being Disheartened

He continues with the blessing of being disheartened. He continues and says, "Blessed are you who weep now, for you shall laugh." What's He talking about? He's talking about disheartened, because you weep at your own potential and capacity to sin. You mourn as you take inventory of what you are capable of. You look at yourself through the eyes of Jesus and you go, "Ugh." This is what nailed Jesus to the cross; the stinking attitude, the words that I speak. We say, "Oh, I didn't mean to say that. It just slipped." No, it was there all the time. We have to weep and mourn for those things.

The Blessing of Being Detested

Then there is the blessing of being detested. When He says, in verse 22, "Blessed are you when men hate you, and when they exclude you, and revile you, and cast out your name as evil, for the Son of Man's sake. Rejoice in that day and leap for joy! For indeed your reward is great in Heaven, for in like manner their fathers did to the prophets."

What do you mean detested? You're unliked. You're made fun of. You're derided because you crave for holiness in your life. You crave for holiness in your attitude. You crave for holiness in your thinking. You crave for holiness in the way you speak. You crave for holiness in the way you treat people. You will be detested for that. You might ask, "How?" Well first of all, their reaction. When you crave this type of holiness you're going to have a reaction on the part of people around you. Your family will be the first one.

Their Reaction

In Luke 6:22 He mentions three particular reactions that they will have. Believe it or not they will hate you. You will lose friends; you will not be popular, and they will exclude you. Young people enjoy being accepted and included in the crowd, but when you live like the Kingdom culture, they will exclude you. They will call you odd, and want nothing to do with you. They will revile you; that means they will speak evil of you and make up things and they will cast your name as evil.

You need to ask yourself something: have I experienced this type of reaction? Their reaction. Secondly, what should your response be when they hate you, exclude you, revile you, and cast your name as evil? Jesus said, "Rejoice! Leap for joy!" Those two things. The first thing you do when they are doing all that to you is rejoice. Get happy! Somebody noticed Jesus in you. Somebody noticed that you march to the beat of a different drum. You're distinctively different. You're not like everybody else; you're not supposed to be everybody else; you have the culture of the Kingdom and you leap for joy. You thank God; you don't go to prayer meetings and say, "Please pray for me. They're picking on me." You ought to be happy, they noticed that you're saved, sanctified, and filled with the Holy Spirit.

Your Reason

What's your reason for rejoicing and leaping? Look what He says in the text, your reward in Heaven is great. First of all, He says great reward in Heaven. What does that mean? It means that Heaven takes notice when you suffer for His sake. Heaven takes notice when you dare to be different. Heaven's taking notes. Heaven's got the best videoing equipment in the universe and while you may weep now, you're going to rejoice later. You might as well start rejoicing now! What's your reason? Wow, they persecuted me like the prophets. I stand in the company of Daniel. I stand in the company of Hosea. I stand in the company of John the Baptist. I stand with Malachi. I stand with all the prophets. Hallelujah! Not a bad company to be put down with.

Unusual Barriers

Then you see unusual barriers. **Luke 6:24-26**, He talks a couple of things over here but let me just say this main thing: He uses the word woe, woe, and woe. Let me tell you the Lord's woes are aimed at things that people covet but that are, in reality, an encumbrance to your spiritual life. What does that mean? A stumbling block; something you trip over. A lot of people are wanting all kinds of things and they don't' even know what they are wanting. The Lord looks at it and says, "Woe! You better be careful!" Careful with what you ask for. If you ask for anything, ask for wisdom. Be like Solomon. He could have had the riches of the world and he asked for wisdom. We need wisdom. The opposite of wisdom is to walk like a fool. A fool is somebody who doesn't want to be corrected. Young lady, don't look to marry a guy, look to marry a man of

God. If a guy doesn't like to be corrected, he's a fool. I don't care how old he is or how much money he has.

Those Who Are Prosperous

The Lord begins with verse 24, "Woe to you who are rich, for you have received your consolation." He is speaking to those who are prosperous in this life. Is there anything wrong with prosperity? No, no, no. I am saying, when you live for it. You just live to count your money and look at your stocks every day. Oh they went down and oh they went up! Oh, how much I have and oh my 401k! Stop! Stop! There's more to life than money!

Let me give you a powerful prophecy by the Lord's brother James. In **James 5:1-6** he prophesies that it is the rich who oppress. It is the rich who oppress. He says, "Come now, **you** rich, weep and howl for your miseries that are coming upon **you**! Your riches are corrupted, and your garments are moth-eaten. Your gold and silver are corroded, and their corrosion will be a witness against you and will eat your flesh like fire. You have heaped up treasure in the last days." This is in the context of the last days, the day we are living in now. "Indeed the wages of the laborers who mowed your fields, which you kept back by fraud, cry out; and the cries of the reapers have reached the ears of the Lord of Sabaoth. You have lived on the earth in pleasure and luxury; you have fattened your hearts as in a day of slaughter. You have condemned, you have murdered the just; he does not resist you."

This, in my opinion, is speaking of the Illuminati, the international bankers, the Bilderbergs, the Council on Foreign Relations, and the secret super rich who invisibly rule the world and are commited to establishing a one world government! Your day is coming! Your day of manipulating elections, your day of controlling things from behind the scenes is coming to an end because if you don't repent, you who hide in secrecy with all of your secret signs and everything else, you will end up in hell unless you repent of your sins to the Lord Jesus Christ.

A lesson from **1 Timothy 6:6-10** is discontentment and straying from the faith. He warns these super rich and all of us because, the people who want money are the ones who are broke: always buying lottery tickets; always hoping for things. Never invest money that you can't afford to lose. He says in **1 Timothy 6:6-10**, "Now godliness with contentment is great gain." You see that Millennials? Be content with what you have. Don't be bothering your parents about what you don't have; focus on what you do have. "For we brought nothing into **this** world, **and it is** certain we can carry nothing out." You know I've done a lot of funerals and I've never seen a dead guy bring anything out of this world or a dead woman. You take nothing with you. "And having food and clothing, with these we shall be content."

Even if McDonald's runs out of fries and ketchup, be content. "But those who desire to be rich fall **into** temptation and a snare, and into many foolish and harmful lusts which drown men in destruction and perdition. For the love of money is a root of all **kinds of** evil, for which some have strayed from the faith in their greediness, and pierced themselves through with many sorrows."

I've seen a lot of people leave wills to their children who never loved them. They only cared about the money, and then they fight for the inheritance. But we need a balance. If there's a choice between poverty and prosperity; give me prosperity, but prosperity with the Kingdom of culture attitude: prosperity that I can use to spread the

Great Commission. The balance is **Proverbs 10:22**; God's blessings prosper us. The scripture says, "The blessing of the Lord makes one rich, and he adds no sorrow with it."

Deuteronomy 8:18. I stand on that scripture. The Bible says, "for it is He (the Lord God) who gives you the power to get wealth that He may establish His covenant, which means that God gives you riches so that you can fulfill the Great Commission not so that you can live high on the hog. Prosperity is for distribution not accumulation. Prosperity is not so that you can have 10 cars, eight fur coats, and excess materialism. Prosperity is so that you can give to the widow and her orphan children, give to missions, spread the gospel, and get millions of people saved.

That's why God wants prosperity and He warns the people who have the money in **1 Timothy 6:17-19**, be you rich in good works. Be ready to give. Be willing to share.

Those who are pleased with this life. If you talked to them they act like everything is fine. "How are you doing?" "Fine man. Everything's cool. Everything's wonderful."

Luke 6:25 says, "Woe to you who are full, for you shall hunger." Kingdom culture says this; you see this is spiritual contentment. This is, "I'm fine. Everything's fine. I'm doing great man. I'm in good health, I'm this, and I'm that."

Are you "fine"? You are not fine. For when we hear Jesus speaking up on the mountain, He is warning, first of all, you have no spiritual hunger. Woe to you because you're not fine, you have no spiritual hunger. It's only the people who are desperate for God's Words and desperate to live right with God. Those are the ones who are fine. I hear the words of the Holy Spirit saying, "They had no appetite for Godly things. Never buying Christian movies, never buying Christian things and if they go to a Christian bookstore they buy all the little trinkets, little toys, and the things like that. Never opening up a book. Never realizing that readers are leaders. Wouldn't even think of buying a commentary or a good devotion."

Those Who Live for Pleasure

Then He says this, "Woe to those who live for pleasure in this life." Luke 6, the second part, says, "Woe to you who laugh now, for you shall mourn and weep." Woe to you who live for fun, entertainment, and games. Woe to you who live for partying. Woe to you who live for that. I want to prophesy to you that I hear the words of Jesus now speaking this saying, "Listen, you care more about football than how many souls are going to get saved next week. You care more about your television, novels, all of those things, having fun, and having a good time."

I'm all in favor of having a good time, but you know what, most of the time I reflect on those who are dying and going to hell. We ought to live to promote His Kingdom. I'm the first one who likes to play board games and have fun and everything, but life is a lot more than that. He talks about those who are popular in life. When you're young, you want to be accepted. When you're young, you want to be popular; you don't want to be rejected.

Those Who Want Popularity

Here's a message for you, **Luke 6:26**, "Woe to you when all men speak well of you, for so did their fathers to the false prophets."

You like when people speak well of you; nobody likes to be put down. It's human nature but I hear the warning of the Lord saying, if all people praise us, not some. He said, "Woe to you if all men speak well of you."

It is perfectly natural to desire people to like what one preaches, but we must realize with Jesus, you either loved Him or you hated Him. But if all people praise us then we have not convicted their conscience. We've been playing the game along with them. We laugh at the dirty jokes, the men look at a beautiful woman and say, "Garcia, what do you think?" "Yeah, yeah man she's good looking." You better open up your mouth sir. You better tell them, "I love Jesus, I have a ring on, and I love my wife."

I am not looking at any woman but my wife. Stop trying to live to please other people! If all people praise us then we have not denounced their favorite sins. If all people praise us then you can talk about what's popular. You know the world; their favorite word is tolerance, and telling the truth is considered hatred.

I love the adulterer, but I love him enough to take him from the path of hell into Heaven. I love the fornicator, but I love him enough to say, "No ring, no thing. You need to get married!" I love the gay and lesbian people; I love them enough to tell them you were not born that way. God says you were not born that way and if you keep living that way, you're going to go to hell and you need to repent. That's real love. I'm not going to sit there on a talk show or sit there in the cafeteria and agree with the people who say, "Well, they were born that way. I don't want to rock the boat." You had better rock the boat!

We need to say, "No. In my love for you, I've got to tell you the truth. I've got to tell you that you weren't born that way. If God says it's wrong, how could then He make you born that way? If God says it's wrong, God said, I believe it, and that settles it." I have Paul's conviction when he says, have I therefore become your enemy because I tell you the truth?" **Galatians 4:16**

If all people praise us all the time, we are in danger of endorsing their sins by our silence. It is the unsaved, relativistic society that talks about Christians being intolerant. They call us intolerant, but they don't tolerate our Christianity. They call us intolerant but when we say, "Jesus is the way, the truth, and the life no man comes to God except through Him. As a result, they don't want to tolerate us. But I have a God who will tell you today there is only one name that is written in Heaven and earth by which we shall be saved: Jesus, Jesus, Jesus." **Acts 4:12**

Unusual Behavior

We need to have a Kingdom culture as the Lord continues to open up His mouth and shock the audience and now He talks about unusual behavior. He begins to talk about behavior like nobody ever talked. **Verses 27-29,** He first talks about have unusual behavior towards our foes. That means enemies. Well, if he's an enemy, you kill him right? No, no, no. You don't kill him.

Love Your Enemy

He says, "But I say to you who hear: love your enemies, do good to those who hate you, bless those who curse you, and pray for those who spitefully use you. To him who strikes you on the one cheek, offer the other also. And from him who takes away your cloak, do not withhold your tunic either."

What He's saying here is I want you to love your enemy. Anybody can love a friend. It takes Kingdom culture to love an enemy. How do you love an enemy? Respond with a good attitude. When they come hateful towards you, you come loving back to them. Respond with a good attitude. Please understand, the reason he's so ornery and is the enemy is because there is a shortage of God in their life. They're bound and they're blind. Then respond with good works. You need to respond with good works. You talk about me, I'm going to buy you lunch. I'm going to send you flowers. I'm going to help pay one of your bills.

Look what the Holy Spirit says through the Apostle Paul in **Romans 12:19-21**, "Beloved, do not avenge yourselves, but rather give place to wrath; for it is written, 'Vengeance is Mine, I will repay,' says the Lord. Therefore, if your enemy is hungry, feed him; if he is thirsty, give him a drink; for in so doing you will heap coals of fire on his head. Do not be overcome by evil, but overcome evil with good."

Where did the expression "Heap coals of fire on his head" come from? In New Testament times, it was thought that if an enemy is giving you a hard time and he is out of coals, he is out of something that you have, you fill your coal bins and you carry it near your head. Then you call him and he says, "What do you want?" Your response: I came to bring you coal and as you give it, you place it on his shoulder, and you are putting coals of fire on his head. You're talking about me and I'm keeping your children warm. You are talking about me and I am praying for you.

Lift Your Up Enemy

Love your enemy and then lift up your enemy. Lift him up. I want to put him down. No, no, no. **Luke 6:28** "Bless those who curse you, and pray for those who spitefully use you." How do you lift up your enemy? The natural thing is to punch them in the face. The natural thing is to unfriend them on Facebook. Beep. That's it. First of all, by blessing them. Blessing is when you speak good things into their life. Blessing is when you say I pray that the Lord prospers you and blesses you. I once heard Jack Hayford say, "My words create my world." So let your words be creative rather than destructive.

The Holy Spirit spoke through Paul in **Ephesians 4:29**, don't let any corrupt communication come out of your mouth but that which edifies, lifts up, and blesses.

Romans 12:14 says, "Bless those who persecute you," and when that shocks you he says I'm going to say it again, "Bless and do not curse." When you curse somebody is when you pronounce and say negative things about them and negative things are again prophetic. **1 Peter 3:9** "Not returning evil for evil or reviling for reviling, but on the contrary blessing, knowing that you were called to this, that you may inherit a blessing." You were called to be a blessing. You were called to speak blessing that you may inherit a blessing. If I speak blessing, I inherit a blessing. Did you get that? What goes around comes around. If I want a blessing, I speak blessing. I'm going to pray for them; Father, get a hold of them and give them a dream of hell that they're going there in Jesus' name.

How about praying **Ephesians 1:17-19**: Father, I lift up Garcia to you. I pray that the eyes of his understanding would be made open that you would grant him the spirit of wisdom and revelation. God, open up his horizons and let him see what he's doing. And then by having compassion for them. Realize they are bound by sin, they are going to hell, and they need Jesus. That's why they're behaving like that. They're not behaving like that because they had a bad upbringing. They're not behaving like that because they grew up in a housing project. They're behaving like that because the devil got a hold of them just like he had a hold of you. Love your enemy, lift your enemy and now let your enemy.

Luke 6:29 reads, "To him who strikes you on the one cheek, offer the other also. And from him who takes away your cloak, do not withhold your tunic either."

This was written to a zealous people wanting to be free of Roman occupation. They were called zealots and Jesus didn't come to set people free politically. He came to set people free spiritually. He could care less if they were under Caesar but a Roman soldier if he slapped you in your face, you better not give him an attitude or the next thing his sword went right through you; you were dead.

He's saying, "Get all of these thoughts of rebelling and retaliating against the Romans out of your mind. You need to retaliate against the sin in your life!" Jesus later authorized the right of self-defense. I am absolutely amazed when I travel the world and I speak to people that say, "If somebody breaks into my house they are going to rape my wife, I'll have to turn the cheek." No! God called men to defend their wife and children.

Luke 22:35-38 tells us how Jesus feels about self-defense, "'When I sent you without money bag, knapsack, and sandals, did you lack anything?' So they said, 'Nothing.' Then He said to them, 'But now, he who has a money bag, let him take it, and likewise a knapsack; and he who has no sword, let him sell his garment and buy one." In our language: you have right to self-defense. That's what He's saying. "'For I say to you that this which is written must still be accomplished in Me:'" He was numbered with the transgressors. Do you know what He is saying here? I've got to be killed. I'm leaving the earth. You all are going to be without Me. "'For the things concerning Me have an end.' So they said, 'Lord, look, here are two swords.' And

He said to them, 'It is enough.'"

Pastor, when they traveled, did one of them have a sword? Yes. You know why? When you go on the Jericho Road, you will be mugged. When they see one of you with a sword, they leave you alone. You have a right to defend yourself.

3 Rules for Self-Defense

This is the number one reason why men don't want to get saved: They fear not being able to defend themselves or their family. There are three rules for self-defense because I want to teach you how to live and ladies pay very close attention because some of us are so filled with the Spirit that we don't look around when you leave Walmart on a dark night, parked in an obscure corner.

Detect

Number one, detect. Be aware and discern. You don't walk to your car, by yourself, in a dark alley saying, "The angels of God, I call you to be here!" You won't need the angels if you have wisdom. If you have wisdom, you will wait for somebody to walk with you.

Disarm

Number two, disarm. I'm talking about verbally. Like verbal judo. You need to disarm people. Hey man, why'd you cut in front of me? Hey, I'm very sorry; I'm not looking for any trouble. Hey, you spilled my coffee! Listen, I'll pay for another cup, okay? I'm going to turn around, I'm going to leave, and I don't want any trouble. You're not a punk because you do that; you have wisdom. Fools say, "What? You picking on me? Let's get it on!" and the result is a violent encounter that could have been avoided!

Hebrews 12:14 "Pursue peace with all people, and holiness, without which no one will see the Lord."

Defend

Number three, defend. If you have to defend yourself, please only as a last resort. If physically attacked and you're in danger, use measured response. Any officer, any policeman will tell you the same. If a drunk said, "Hey you...I'm going to..." you don't put them in a chokehold. That's not measured response; that's a fool's response. You don't barrage them with all kinds of things because they looked at your wife. If somebody looks at your wife, keep walking. If they make comments, keep walking. Only if you are attacked, do you respond.

How about when they steal from you? "Oh Pastor, I don't like somebody taking my things. I work so hard. Whose things are they? I thought they belonged to God, you know."

He says in **Luke 6:29b,** "And from him who takes away your cloak, do not withhold your tunic either. Give to everyone who asks of you. And from him who takes away your goods do not ask them back."

This was written primarily to stop resistance to Roman occupation. **Matthew 5:40-42** "If anyone wants to sue you and take away your tunic, let him have your cloak also. Whoever compels you to go one mile, go with him two. Give to him who asks you, and from him who wants to borrow from you do not turn away."

I am not talking about somebody stalking you, oppressing you, purposely pursuing you, causing havoc on Facebook and online, and following your children and threatening them. I am not speaking of that. I had a business person tell me, does that mean if somebody ran up my bill and now doesn't want to pay...I said, you now take them to court because they are not acting like a Christian. I am not talking about the widow woman who has medical bills and can't pay you back. Hey man, just write it off.

This was written primarily to stop resistance to Roman occupation. Now, what you do is appeal to the police and authorities for they are appointed by God to protect you. A lot of people say I'm not calling the police. Well, why not? God anoints police. Please remember this the next time they pull you over and the police car lights are behind you. Don't start speaking in tongues and then cursing them.

Romans 13:3-4 "For rulers are not a terror to good works, but to evil. Do you want to be unafraid of the authority [that's speaking of police]? Do what is good, and you will have praise from the same. For he is God's minister to you for good. But if you do evil, be afraid; for he does not bear the sword in vain; for he is God's minister."

You need to look at police differently. Kingdom people look at police as ministers to be respected. Well, are there bad police officers? Yes, and there are bad ministers too, but as a whole you look at them as ministers, there to help you.

Luke 6:30-40, "Give to everyone who asks of you. And from him who takes away your goods do not ask them back. And just as you want men to do to you, you also do to them likewise. But if you love those who love you, what credit is that to you? For even sinners love those who love them. If you do good to those who do good to you, what credit is that to you? For even sinners do the same. If you lend to those from whom you hope to receive back, what credit is that you? For even sinners lend to sinners to receive as much back."

Let me give you *seven* dynamic, powerful insights.

Number one. The actions and works we do now on earth will directly affect how we are rewarded in eternity. That's what Jesus is saying. He goes on to say, "And your reward will be great."

Number two. He says, the actions and works we do now on earth should be exemplary and proof that we're saved. We ought to show proof that we're saved. Look at what He says in **Luke 6:35**, "But love your enemies, do good, and lend, hoping for nothing in return; and your reward will be great, and you will be sons of the Most High." Or daughters of the Most High. You prove your daughtership and your sonship by the way you treat people who don't treat you good.

Number three. We should be kind to the unthankful and evil. You want me to be kind to that horrible person.? Yes, do not let his/her behavior affect the way that you are going to respond to them. Just because they're cold, calculating, and unkind doesn't mean you have to change your attitude, demeanor, or actions.

Number four. We should supply people's need when it is within our ability and regardless of whether they are friend or enemy. We read that before: if you only love people who love you, what credit is that to you? If you only give money to people who are going to pay you back, what credit is that to you? May I make a suggestion to fathers and grandfathers: if you give money to your kids don't have a long memory. Don't say, "Son, it's been two years and I gave you this amount of money." You will put your son under such condemnation. At the same time, train him up while he's young to pay his bills and to be a man of his word. Fools don't pay back their debts.

Number five. In life the things we do for others will eventually come back to us. Isn't that true? **Luke 6:31** – "And just as you want men to do to you, you also do to them likewise." You have to remember that. If I plant a seed, I'm going to get a harvest. So, let's plant good seeds.

Number six. Live a life of mercy. Mercy is what you give to someone that doesn't deserve it. On that day when I stand before God, when you stand before God, don't you want mercy? Live a life of forgiveness. You need to walk in forgiveness. You need to plan forgiveness.

Number seven. We can only lead others to the extent that we ourselves are following Christ. Remember this when you're raising your son, your daughter, and your grandchildren. I hear Jesus saying in **Luke 6:39-40**, "And He spoke a parable to them: 'Can the blind lead the blind? Will they not both fall into a ditch? A disciple is not above his teacher, but everyone who is perfectly trained will be like his teacher.'" Your daughter will be like you; the acorn doesn't fall far from the tree. Maybe you weren't really thinking; maybe you were acting foolish when your daughter said, "Dad, your boss is on the phone." "Tell him I'm not here." You just taught her to lie. You just taught her the deception that you can tell a white lie.

Think about your faults; we all have them. **Luke 6:41** – "Why do you look at the speck in your brother's eye, but do not perceive the plank in your own eye? Or how can you say to your brother, 'Brother, let me remove the speck that is in your eye,' when you yourself do not see the plank that is in your own eye? Hypocrite!"

In the matter of criticism, before I criticize you, let me take an x-ray of my actions and my motives. Let me take an inventory and even if I haven't done it, I know that deep down inside that I am very capable of that. So just because

I see your mistake doesn't mean I'm not next. Then there is the matter of corruption. We really need to take inventory of this towards our own faults. If you are wise today, you will take heed. You will check yourself out and ask God for His mercy and His grace because without the Holy Spirit, we can't do any of this.

Luke 6:43-44 reads: "For a good tree does not bear bad fruit, nor does a bad tree bear good fruit. For every tree is known by its own fruit. For men do not gather figs from thorns, nor do they gather grapes from a bramble bush."

We do what we do because of what we are. For years, psychologists have been teaching that we're a product of our environment.

The truth is that we are all basically sinful when we we're born; we have a propensity to rebel and do not like anyone telling us what to do. It is basic selfishness and rebellion until Jesus cleans us up. We are what we are because of who we are. **Luke 6:43** says, a good tree can only bear good fruit. I don't know about you, but I've been a good sinner. When I sinned, I did it well. I want to do good things for God.

The mouth will always speak and reveal the desire, priorities, and condition of the heart. **Matthew 12:32** talks about out of the abundance of the heart, the mouth speaks. It didn't slip; it was there all the time.

Jesus said three invaluable, powerful truths that talk to you and I about ourselves because they reveal that there are really three kinds of Christians in the church and three kinds of people in the world.

The Tragedy of Contradictory Faith

The first one is the tragedy of a contradictory faith. These are deceived people. It says in **Luke 6:46**, "But why do you call Me 'Lord, Lord,' and not do the things which I say?" That's interesting, we give Him the right title but then we don't give Him the respect behind it. How can you call a man father when you treat him disrespectfully? Don't say "Mom" and then not listen to her. Mom implies respect. This is a tragedy. These people come to church every week but their life and their mouth contradicts the very God that they say that they serve. They say, "Lord, Lord," there's only one time that I know of that you use the double name, the double title, and that is in an emergency. For example, if there was a fire in the church, people wouldn't say, "Oh there's a fire." They'll say, "Fire! Fire!" Everybody will say, "Where? Where?"

"There! There!" "Let's go! Let's go!" Human beings use the double title when there's an emergency. He's saying, "Why do you call me Lord when you have an emergency, and then, after I take care of it, you tell me, now I'll take over? You are contradicting in your faith.

The Triumph of a Correct Faith

Secondly, the triumph of a correct faith. Here's where you want to be. You want to be discipled. You don't want to be deceived; you want to be discipled. In verse 46, they were deceived. You want to be discipled. In Luke 6:47-48, Jesus said, "Whoever comes to Me, and hears My sayings and does them, I will show you whom he's like. He is like a man building a house, who dug deep and laid the foundation."

The foundation is your decisions. The house is your life. He puts His decisions on the rock of the Word of Godor Jesus. Notice it says he "dug deep." We must dig past whatever stands between us and obeying God's Word

147

with the help of the Holy Spirit. For example, we must dig past self will, unforgiveness, rebellion, lust, etc. Then Jesus tells us, "And when the flood arose, the flood comes and it beats vehemently against us. The flood represents crises and emergencies. Jesus taught that the flood of crises will come. You cannot duck them; they are unavoidable. This parable says the flood waters hit the house, but couldn't even shake it for it was founded on the rock. That's where you want to be. You can crisis proof your life by digging past your self will, by the grace of God; and base your decisions on God's Word.

The Test of a Confessed Faith

Thirdly, see **Luke 6:49** which speaks of a defeated person. Unfortunately, a vast number of church attenders are defeated people. They believe in Jesus. They've even confessed Him. They've even prayed and got very emotional, but they never dug past their self will with God's help. It says, he who heard and did nothing. See? He's foolish; he heard and did nothing. He came, he heard, but he failed to be a doer of the Word of God. **James 1:22** It says when the stream beat vehemently against that house, immediately it fell and the ruin of the house was great. **Luke 6:49**

Which one of these three represents you? Do you go to pieces when an emergency comes? If you do, you're probably number three.

CHAPTER SEVEN

The Parable of the Kingdom:
THE ANSWER KEY

"Another parable He put forth to them, saying: "The Kingdom of Heaven is like a mustard seed, which a man took and sowed in his field, which indeed is the least of all the seeds; but when it is grown it is greater than the herbs and becomes a tree, so that the birds of the air come and nest in its branches." **Matthew 13:31-32**

Then He said, "To what shall we liken the Kingdom of God? Or with what parable shall we picture it? It is like a mustard seed which, when it is sown on the ground, is smaller than all the seeds on earth; but when it is sown, it grows up and becomes greater than all herbs, and shoots out large branches, so that the birds of the air may nest under its shade." **Mark 4:30-32**

Then He said, "What is the Kingdom of God like? And to what shall I compare it? It is like a mustard seed, which a man took and put in his garden; and it grew and became a large tree, and the birds of the air nested in its branches." **Luke 13:18-19**

Key Take Away: Churches, like people, can have the appearance of being Christian, but in reality deny Jesus by false doctrines and false living.

In **Matthew 13**, Jesus gives a couple of parables of the Kingdom. Unfortunately, we in the West don't understand what the word parable means because it's an Eastern term. It's a farming term and I'm going to do our best to try and clarify that.

The Lord is speaking in front of a huge crowd. He has their undivided attention. He had already given the parable of the sower. He had already explained; I don't speak direct to them; I speak in parables or stories. We are going to get into that and the reason He does that is because God wants to distinguish the hungry from the curious. God wants to distinguish those who are religious from those who really want a relationship. Jesus did that by parables. But there is something strange here even before we look into anything else. A mustard seed does not produce a tree, it produces a shrub, which is like a large plant. Yet the parable says that this shrub became a huge tree. As a matter of fact, the word for tree there is oak tree. Something is not right. His listeners are hearing Him and saying something's not right over here; this is abnormal; He's talking about something abnormal and so He has their undivided attention.

Unfortunately, we in the West, we think a seed, shrub, tree it's all the same thing. It's not! Jesus is talking about the Church and the future of the Church and what's going to happen in the Church.

Churches, like people, can have the appearance of being Christian but in reality deny Jesus by false doctrines and false living.

Doctrine has become a bad word nowadays. It's not a bad word. The Gospel is full of doctrine and doctrine tells you how to live. You should understand this. Have you driven on a highway recently? What are the lines called? Those lines are boundaries and in the gospel of the Kingdom you have boundaries. Here's the beauty of God: you have boundaries by the sovereignty of God, but then you are free to drive in whatever lane you want. So you can do what you want as long as you stay within the boundaries. If you didn't have boundaries, you would have mortal accidents. You and I need boundaries of the Word of God. We have to have boundaries.

Let's look at the comparison in the parable. This is actually what you call a similitude. A similitude is something that is like something in reality. It's similar to something in reality. The first thing we want to look at as we are hearing Jesus speak is the term that He's using. He's using a term that does not coincide with Western culture, especially in America. The term that He uses is first of all, parable. We in America don't understand what the word parable means. We just think it's a story. Parable comes from two words; it comes from the word *para*, which means alongside. It means to come beside or to come alongside of something. For example, paralegal is someone who comes alongside a lawyer. Para church is an organization like Teen Challenge or Youth with a Mission; they come alongside of the Church. Paratrooper is someone who drops out of an airplane and comes alongside the infantry.

In America, we just don't understand that. Then comes the word *bole*, which means to toss; it means to throw. For example, bowling, you toss a ball. When you put that together a parable therefore becomes a supernatural story laid alongside a natural story. What does that mean? It means an earthly story. It's an earthly story with a Heavenly meaning. The whole world knows the parable of the prodigal son. It probably happened and every culture knows that. It's an earthly story, but it has a Heavenly meaning of the love of a father for two sons that didn't really deserve his love. Then the Lord develops the topic that He is talking about and He's got His audience listening. I want you to hear the Lord and let's distinguish the phrases that He uses.

Let's look at the distinction of the phrases that He uses because in Matthew. He says "Kingdom of Heaven," and Mark and Luke say "Kingdom of God." Well, which is it?

First of all, the Kingdom of Heaven is where God lives in the Heavenlies. In fact, He died and went to Heaven. It's way deep in space. Christian scientists call that the black hole. It's way out there! But the Kingdom of God, is the government and rulership in the life of the Christian. When He says Kingdom of God, He is saying, "I want to rule your life and I want to govern your life." I want to be like those highway lanes; you can choose your clothes, you can choose your food, but you have to stay within the lanes. You've got to stay in there. You can't just live your life the way you want to live. God says, "I want to rule you. I want to govern you." Many Christians think that as long as I say, "Jesus, forgive me of my sins," I'm going to go to Heaven. It's more than that.

If you look at **Romans 10:8-9**, Lordship comes before repentance. If you confess that Jesus is Lord, you will be saved. Lordship is from the very beginning. If He's not Lord of everything, He's not Lord of anything. As quoted in *When Heaven Invades Earth*, "As the Kingdom of God confronts sin, forgiveness is given and change comes to the nature that has only known how to sin. When His rule collides with disease, people are healed. When it runs into the demonized, they are set free. The

Kingdom message's nature provides salvation for the whole man—spirit, soul, and body. That is the gospel of Jesus Christ."[28]

Kingdom of God means something more. To quote Bill Johnson "Look at the word Kingdom—*king-dom*. It refers to the king's domain, implying authority and lordship. Jesus came to offer the benefits of His world to all who surrender to His rule. The realm of God's dominion, that realm of all sufficiency, is the realm called the Kingdom. The benefits of His rule were illustrated through His works of forgiveness, deliverance, and healing."[29] And the works of the Kingdom of God continues through His church: you and me. **John 14:12**

This is what the apostle meant in **1 Corinthians 2** when he said, "I didn't come to you with fancy words but I came to you in the demonstration of the power of the Holy Spirit that your faith would not be in words but in power. **1 Corinthians 2:4-5**

That's what he meant in **1 Corinthians 4:20** for the Kingdom of God is not just words, it's power and we should be known as a people of power. But let me give you a fourth one: I want you to know that the Kingdom of God and the Kingdom of Heaven are used interchangeably. Many times these two terms are used interchangeably so you can hardly tell what you're seeing. You have to really listen closely because they are used interchangeably. For example, we read in Matthew he used Kingdom of Heaven and then in Mark and Luke he used Kingdom of God. He moves into a description. He gives a description of the parable and His listeners kind of knew, but we Americans don't know and so let's look at this description.

A General Description

I want you first of all to consider a general description of what He's talking about. The Kingdom of God is the empire of God, the dominion of God, and the rule of God. Jesus is saying His kingdom will grow numerically. Before you get all excited, big doesn't mean right. I'm giving you a hint that I'm setting you up. It's going to be so big that a shrub is going to turn like an oak tree and have branches. The last mustard seed plant I saw has twigs; it doesn't have branches. The Lord is talking about something that's going to be massive in size. At that time, there were only Jews and Gentiles. Right now, if you're not a Jew and you're not a Muslim then you're considered a Christian, but not really. He gives a general description.

Mark 1:15 reads, "And saying, 'The time is fulfilled, and the Kingdom of God is at hand. Repent, and believe in the gospel.'" **Acts 28:30-31** – "Then Paul dwelt two whole years in his own rented house, and received all who came to him, preaching the Kingdom of God and teaching the things which concern the Lord Jesus Christ with all confidence, no one forbidding him."

An Adversarial Description

I want to focus in on the adversarial description. What the Lord is trying to aim at is that God's Kingdom will be opposed by Satan and his Kingdom. There's going to be a fight. For example, **1 Corinthians 16:9**, Paul preaching says, "For a great and effective door has opened to me, and there are many adversaries." You have to fight to plant churches. It's a fight to win souls!

In **Ephesians 6:12** we're told that we don't wrestle against people. Your battle is not against personalities;

your battle is against invisible being, against powers and principalities, spiritual hosts of wickedness.

Don't put a face to the fight. You've got a problem with your boss, somebody on your job, somebody in your school? It's a spirit behind them. So don't curse people and say, "What an idiot!" It's the spirits behind them. Your battle is not against flesh and blood; your battle is against invisible beings in the Heavenlies and here on earth called demons.

It's what Peter says in **1 Peter 5:8**, "Be sober, be vigilant; because your adversary the devil walks about like a roaring lion, seeking whom he may devour." Resist him steadfast in the faith. Let me tell you something, the devil devours people. I lived in Africa for a season and people say old lions roar because they don't have teeth. Not so! An old lion is still capable of killing.

But how does Satan oppose the Church? He does it three ways:

1. *Persecution.*

He will resist; he will fight the Church and you know what that means. They will threaten you; you get fired from a job. In the Middle East, ISIS is beheading children if the parents do not deny Jesus as Lord and Savior. If you ever find yourself in that situation, it is the grace of God that will strengthen you to die for your faith. Do not ever deny Jesus as Lord and Savior even to save your son or daughter. God will give you faith. God will give you strength by His Grace. Don't make an emotional, temporary decision. You will die immediately and you know what? You will have a martyr's crown for all of eternity, a badge of honor on the other side. Nothing is worth denying Jesus. We do not have a fear of death. **Hebrews 2:14**

2. *Contradiction.*

Satan tried to persecute the Church, but the Church kept growing. He tried to kill them, but the Church kept growing. Next, Satan used the weapon of false doctrine to contradict the teachings of the church. One of the first false doctrines was the doctrine of the Nicolaitans. You read about this group in **Revelation 2:6 and verse 15.** In **Revelation 2:6** one church wasn't doing good, but Jesus tells them one thing you've done well is you've resisted the doctrine of the Nicolaitans. But to the church at Pergamos He says, you are espousing the Nicolaitans. As a matter of fact, there's a lady called Jezebel in your midst and she is a Nicolaitan. Who was Nicolas? This came from a Spirit-filled deacon named Nicolas that you find in Acts 6. Do you think that they appointed some pervert to be a deacon? You can begin well, but you can end bad. This man came up with a doctrine that they later named after him. In theology, we call it Antinomianism: a false belief that one can morally live as he pleases because we are under grace. When we're saved and we're born again our spirits are born again, but in our flesh we can do what we want. So the Nicolaitans would eat meat offered to idols, they would attend orgies, they committed adultery and fornication regularly?

Do we see that today? Yes, we do, it's called the doctrine of hyper-grace. We're saved by grace, hallelujah! We don't have to repent anymore; we repented once. If you want to get high and take a few shots of whiskey, it's okay. We're saved by the grace of God. If you have lust for a woman and you happen to fall, don't worry about it. Just tell God you're sorry and keep right on going. Hyper-Grace teaches Jesus already died for your future sins so there is no need to repent.

This thinking has led the Church to think you can be saved and be an adulterer, a fornicator, a homosexual and it doesn't make a difference. That's called "greasy" grace; that's not grace. Read **Titus 2:11-13** and it says the grace of God has taught us to be unspotted from the world, to stay away from the works of the flesh. So, false doctrine came in.

3. *Infiltration*.

In the years 300, the devil used a Roman Emperor named Constantine. Constantine felt inspired to conquer what many think is a sign of the cross. But it wasn't a sign of the cross; it was a cross with a circle around it. It was an *ansk*. By this sign you'll conquer. *Ansk* is an Egyptian God and what he did was he took all of the Barbarians and he said you're all members of the Church. All you have to do is pledge allegiance to two things: Rome and then give your allegiance to Jesus, but you can keep all your false gods and ungodly practices.

As they passed through they would sprinkle them and that sprinkling made them a Christian. Constantine infiltrated and from then on, persecution ceased. Infiltration stifled the Church and it became weak, godless, and ineffective. In the modern days, around the 1900s a man named Charles Taze Russell came up with the Jehovah's Witness and that has caused so much damage worldwide. Then a false prophet named Joseph Smith came up with the Mormons. He was a Free Mason who had visions and dreams that were demonic. I'm not saying that this group can't be saved, but as an institution, the Roman Catholic Church espouses salvation by works, not by grace and the blood only. It teaches that you pray to saints, when saints are born again Christians. It teaches that Mary is the co-redeemer along with Jesus. It teaches that you need a priest to make confession, when every born again Christian is a priest and can make intercession to God. That institution is being used by the enemy right now to create a one-world government and a one-world religion.

The Roman Catholic Church is helping not the Church, but Christendom to grow. The general description, the adversarial description, and now let's hear Jesus when He gives the distinctive of the phrases. I want you to understand that the Church is not the same as the Kingdom of God or Kingdom of Heaven. While the Church is not the Kingdom of God, it's the most important part of it.

Ephesians 1:10 reads: "That in the dispensation of the fullness of the times He might gather together in one all things in Christ, both which are in Heaven and which are on earth – in Him."

I've read a lot of commentaries on this and compared it with what I felt in the Holy Spirit and I just want you to know that this parable, the words Jesus is speaking to us right now, is very controversial. It has a controversy over four things. Let's break it down.

The Smallness of the Seeds

Number one, the smallness of the seeds. If you were to hold in your hand a mustard seed, you could hardly see it. I mean it is absolutely microscopic.

Matthew 13:31 reads: "The Kingdom of Heaven is like a mustard seed." His listeners are hearing about this tiny little seed that if you sneezed it would blow all over the place. You mean to tell me that this little thing is going to grow into this giant tree, resembling an oak tree, and having branches? Mustard shrubs have twigs not branches. What I love about the smallness of the seed is Luke 17:6.

In **Luke 17:6** Jesus said if you have faith the size of a mustard seed, you can move a giant mulberry tree. That gives me hope friends that little faith can produce great things. He talks about the sowing of the seed.

The Sowing of the Seed

It says in **Matthew 13:31**, "The Kingdom of Heaven is like a mustard seed, which a man took and sowed in is field." Field there is the earth, the world. What does this speak to us? It speaks to us that the Kingdom of God is all about evangelism. You are planting the seed of the gospel. There is no doubt the most liberal interpreter of the parable of the sower; the seed goes out one falls on hard ground, the other shallow ground, the other on thorny ground. The seed is the Word of God and you know what? This is what it's speaking to us: everybody here is a seed sower. Another way of putting it is that everybody here is a seed planter. You are to plant seeds.

The Success of the Seed

Do something good for somebody and then when they say, "How can I repay you?" Say, "Listen to this CD, read this tract, come to church with me next Sunday." There is something you can do to scatter the seed. There is something you can do to preach the gospel and present the gospel of the Kingdom. The success of the seed, this is what gets me nervous. In **Mark 4:32** it says that when "It grows up and becomes greater than all herbs, and shoots out large branches, so that the birds of the air may nest under its shade."

Two insights. The first insight is that Christianity started very small with Christ and His disciples and has amazingly spread throughout the whole world. They even have the gospel in the North Pole and the South Pole. But don't get too happy. Just because there's a church it doesn't mean it's the right church.

You might not like number two. In spite of the innumerable number of Christians that will be saved, let me pause, innumerable means you can't even count it. **Revelation 5:11** says, "Then I looked, and I heard the voice of many angels around the throne, the living creatures, and the elders; and the number of them was ten thousand times ten thousand, and thousands of thousands." You know what that means? You can't count them even if you are careful. But in spite of the innumerable number of Christians that will be saved it appears that in comparison to the amount of people born in history, few will be saved.

There are more people that are going to die and go to hell than are going to die and go to Heaven?

Luke 13:23-30 "Then one said to Him, 'Lord, are there few who are saved?" And He said to them, 'Strive to enter through the narrow gate, for many [in the Greek: majority}, I say to you, will seek to enter and will not be able. When once the Master of the house has risen up and shut the door, and you begin to stand outside and knock at the door, saying, "Lord, Lord, open for us," and He will answer and say to you, "I do not know you, where you are from," then you will begin to say, "We ate and drank in Your presence,'" Let me give the modern application: we went to church, we waved banners, we sang the popular, latest Christian songs, committed a little adultery in between but we did all of that. And He's going to say, "Depart from Me, all you workers of iniquity." Jesus said there will be few saved.

Make sure you are part of the remnant. Make sure you are a part of the few. I want to prophesy to you right now: many of you have unsaved sons and daughters and grandchildren. I decree right now in the name of Jesus. I call them out of darkness; I call them into the light. I call your brothers and your sisters to leave their sin and repent and know Jesus as Lord and Savior. I declare right now that everyone reading this book that their family and friends will be part of the few. I declare that God will give them every chance in the world to give their lives to God.

The Seduction of the Seed

The word "seduce" means fooled. If you get seduced, you get fooled.

Matthew 13:32 "Which indeed is the least of all seeds; but when it is grown it is greater than the herbs and becomes a tree," or in the Greek word an oak tree.

Luke 13:19 "It is like a mustard seed, which a man took and put in his garden; and it grew and became a large tree." Hey, wait a minute, Let's look at five insights. His listeners are saying this doesn't make sense.

Insight Number One. We all have mustard seeds in our yard; it's a great herb, it's a wonderful seasoning, it's just a little plant, it's just a little shrub. What you're saying is that this organization is going to massively grow. This parable should be called the parable of the abnormal mustard seed. There's something strange going on here. It should be the abnormal mustard seed.

Insight Number Two. The mustard plant is a shrub. I don't know what shrub means. A lot of people in America, Western Europe, and Canada think they are Christians because they believe in Jesus. That's weird. To believe in Jesus means that you follow Jesus. To believe in Jesus means that you don't do the sins Jesus talked about. I want to let you in on a secret, the devil believes in Jesus.

Birds don't go to mustard seed trees; they don't like the smell. The Bible is its best interpreter and the law of first mention is right here in the chapter **Matthew 13:4,** "And as he sowed, some seed fell by the wayside; and the birds came and devoured them." **Matthew 13:19** "When anyone hears the word of the Kingdom, and does not understand it, then the wicked one comes and snatches away what was sown in his heart." So, it was the devil who sends the birds.

Insight Number Three. **Luke 8:5** "A sower went out to sow his seed. And as he sowed, some fell by the wayside; and it was trampled down, and the birds of the air devoured it." **Luke 8:12** "Those by the wayside are the ones who hear; then the devil comes and takes away the word out of their hearts." It seems like birds are associated, in the context, with the devil. Well, what exactly are the birds?

First of all, the bird snatches away the good seed in the parable of the sower. We know that.

Secondly, the birds symbolize demons, servants of the prince of the power of the air. The devil controls the atmosphere. **Ephesians 2:2** "In which you once walked according to the course of this world, according to the prince of the power of the air, the spirit who now works in the sons of disobedience."

Thirdly, you may ask, "Pastor, are you saying that the Lord predicted that there would be demonic infiltration of the church in the last days? Absolutely! Keep reading; make sure you're not part of a church that's demonic.

Fourthly, this parable is followed by the parable of the leaven. Leaven means yeast, speaking of impurity and making the bread rise, which speaks of corruption in the Kingdom. Are you saying that Jesus is warning His listeners that there will be corruption in the organization called the Church in the last days? Yes!

Matthew 13:33 says: "The Kingdom of Heaven is like leaven, which a woman took and hid in three measures of meal till it was all leavened."

Luke 13:20-21 reads: "To what shall I liken the Kingdom of God? It is like leaven, which a woman took and hid in three measures." The woman here is the enemy, coming in to infiltrate the Church.

Fifthly, this parable shows the difference between Christendom and the true Church. I told you about the emperor Constantine. Constantine made all of the barbarians Christians provided that they gave allegiance to Rome and believe in Jesus but kept their old beliefs. One of the biggest beliefs was that they can keep the winter solstice, December 21st, and that the man child would be born on the 25th of December. Does that sound familiar? Hint: Jesus was not born in December. The sheep with the shepherds would have frozen out there.

But these beliefs became imbedded and this is why Constantine allowed the so-called Christians to eat meat offered to idols, to believe in dead spirits that one can talk to them, and believe many other false things. There's compromise in the Church my friend. Many Roman Catholics are getting saved. In my opinion the Roman Catholic Church is not part of Christendom because of unscriptural beliefs and practices. For example, why go to a priest in confession when we can go directly to Jesus? There is a priesthood of all believers.

No offense to your upbringing (like mine), but you shall know the truth and the truth will set you free. I hope I have not become your enemy by telling you the truth? **Galationas 4:16** We need to know these things. But in the grace of God, God is saving Jehovah's Witnesses; God is saving Mormons and He's saving Roman Catholics. But I want to warn you the Pope right now is making plans to make a one-world religion, combining all the three major faiths: Judaism, Islam, and Christianity.

What does this mean to you and I? Let me share with you counsel from the parable. There are many churches filled with demons and false doctrines. People have come to me, "Pastor how come we don't have crosses in the church?" You know who has a nice cross? The New Age Church over here, the metaphysical church. Crosses don't make Christians. You need to repent of that religious spirit. The cross is in your heart!

I mentioned earlier, and will rephrase, the great Baptist preacher S.D. Gordon, "Every heart has a throne and a cross. If Jesus is on the throne, self is on the cross. But if self is on the throne, Jesus is on the cross."[30] That's why I don't like crucifixes. He's not dead; He's alive! I thank God for the blood He shed on the cross; but I thank God even more for the resurrection of Jesus. He lives and He empowers us!

Finally, be sure you are born again and are part

of a Bible-believing and preaching church. How do I know what's a Bible-believing and preaching church? Have you ever heard this statement: "Well, you know all churches are the same; it doesn't make a difference which church you go to." Nothing can be further from the truth. There are churches that will send your soul straight to hell and seduce your sons and daughters. You better watch out. The church you go to can dramatically affect where you will spend eternity. There are seven indications that you're in a Bible-based church.

1. They believe the Bible is inspired and inerrant. That means without error. You mean you guys believe that Jonah was swallowed by a whale? I didn't say a whale I said it was a giant fish and yes I do believe that. Men have been found in the belly of a huge fish after three days.

2. They emphasis being saved/born again by the grace of God and the blood of Jesus. Nothing takes away your sins but the blood of Jesus. Good works won't get you saved! One of the tenants of the Roman Catholic Church is that you can be saved by works. Wrong! **Ephesians 1:7** "In Him we have redemption through His blood." **Ephesians 2:8-9** "For by grace you have been saved through faith, and that not of yourselves; it is the gift of God, not of works, lest anyone should boast."

3. Bible-believing churches emphasize evangelism, missions, and altar calls. A Bible church, if they preach that you need to be saved, they will invite people to receive Jesus. Whether in the front or in your seats, but they will invite you to repent of your sins and if you don't do this then you're sending

somebody to hell. We don't preach politically correct, nice messages. Go to a church that does not preach sermonettes to Christianettes. One that the preaching steps on your toes because the preacher wants to see you in Heaven.

4. Bible-believing churches preach conviction, holiness, and righteousness. What does conviction mean? It means you sit there and feel the sting of Holy Spirit conviction that you have sinned and then desire to get right with God.

5. They emphasize the love of God and the fear of God. Anybody have a daddy like me or a mom like me? I love my mom, but let me tell you, her sandal, her reach was never far. I did something wrong – WHACK! My father found out – WHACK! I knew he loved me, but oh how I had a fear of that belt. We fear God's judgments! Too much lovey, lovey and you have what many call "sloppy agape." Too much fear of God and you have condemnation. You need both.

6. Bible-believing churches allow the Holy Spirit and His gifts to move. You want the presence of God. I was with two friends who are Bible School professors just this last week. I just decided to take them out to eat, treated them to a great lunch at Olive Garden. One of them told me this, "I travel the whole of the Southeast. Dave, do you know that the average length of our Assemblies of God churches, Pentecostal, Baptist churches is 65 minutes long at most 75 minutes." That is all people want. They want to get out of church, go running, go boating, go hiking, just go. Jesus, I love You, but hurry up. I want Your healing but hurry

up. I want all that You want within 65 minutes after that, BEEP, your time's up. But they'll stay and watch a football game for three hours and go tail gating for another two hours for their team.

7. They emphasize the soon-coming of Jesus. I've met born again Christians that don't realize that we're in the last days, that there's a real anti-Christ, that there's a real tribulation coming, and that there's a rapture that's going to happen. It's going to happen! Be sure that you are producing the fruit of the Spirit.

Galatians 5:22-23 reads: "love, joy, peace, gentleness, self-control. Be sure to remain in Christ and endure until the end. It's very hard to lose your salvation. God will fight for you but you can walk out on God and lose your salvation. Let me propose some scriptures to you. Do you know that they were writing to the church? When Paul, through the Holy Spirit, was writing to the Colossians."

Colossians 1:21-23 says: "And you, who once were alienated and enemies in your mind by wicked words, yet now He has reconciled in the body of His flesh through death, to present you holy, and blameless, and above reproach in His sight – if indeed you continue in the faith, grounded and steadfast, and are not moved away from the hope of the gospel."

Tell me, would he tell you don't be moved away if it wasn't possible to move away? I didn't ask you if you like it. I'm asking you, what does it say? **Matthew 24:13** "But he who endures to the end shall be saved." Make sure you endure until the end. The Holy Spirit, writing through Paul writes in **1 Corinthians 6:9-10**, "Do you not know that the unrighteous will not inherit the

Kingdom of God." Stop Paul! Stop! We're all saved; we can't lose our salvation! Continue, "Do not be deceived. Neither fornicators, nor idolaters, nor adulterers, nor homosexuals, nor sodomites, nor thieves, nor covetous, nor drunkards, nor revilers, nor extortioners will inherit the Kingdom of God."

Then I love verse 11, "And such were some of you." You know why he's saying this? The Holy Spirit is saying – and the rest of you better not go back to that.

Galatians 5:19-21, the one that nails it is, "Now the works of the flesh are evident, which are: adultery, fornication, uncleanness, lewdness, idolatry, sorcery, hatred, contentions, jealousies, outbursts of wrath, selfish ambitions, dissensions, heresies, envy, murders, drunkenness, revelries, and the like; of which I tell you beforehand, just as I also told you in the time past, that those who practice such things will not inherit the Kingdom of God."

If it was impossible to lose your salvation, why is he writing that to the church in Galatia? The one that nails it all is James the half-brother of Jesus, the head of the church.

James 5:19-20 His epistle went to all churches and he said this, not the difference between verse 19 and verse 20, "Brethren, if anyone among you wanders from the truth." Wanders from the truth. You look up the Greek word wander it means depart. "And someone turns him back, let him know that he who turns a sinner [the brother who became a sinner] from the error of his way will save a soul from death and cover a multitude of sins."

I propose to you that though it is difficult, you can

lose your salvation. Then **2 Thessalonians 2:3**, an event we're seeing right now, "Now brethren, concerning the coming of our Lord Jesus Christ and our gathering together to Him, we ask you, not to be soon shaken in mind or troubled, either by spirit of by word or by letter, as if from us, as though the day of Christ had come. Let no one deceive you by any means; for that day will not come unless the falling away comes first." You can't fall if you weren't standing.

Luke 8:13-15 says they believed for a while but after temptation they fall away. You can only fall if you at one point were standing up. They'll say, "Well, they were never saved." Impossible! Fall means to fall down. In **2 Thessalonians 2:3**, the word "falling away" is *apostasia*, apostasy. Here's the mind blower, the Holy Spirit led me one day to study the word apostasy and go to Matthew chapter nineteen. Did you know that the word divorce in Matthew 19 is the same root word as apostasy in another form, *apostasion*?

When you divorce a wife you apostatize her, you sever ties with her. The falling away will be people who divorce Jesus. When you divorce Jesus, you are no longer married. Many say there's no salvation after that. That might be. I'm just trying to warn you. **Acts 20:31** But I want to end this on two positive notes. Be sure you maintain intimacy with Jesus by maintaining a strong worship and devotional life. Show your love for Jesus. Secondly, when the Holy Spirit convicts you, repent right away, and if He asks you to do something, obey Him!

Ephesians 2:10 tells us, "For we are His workmanship, created in Christ Jesus for good works." What good works are you doing? I want to challenge you – be sure you are involved in ministry. Stay in the area of your assignment and your anointing. If you're anointed to sing, don't try to fix cars. You fix cars? Do everybody a favor and don't sing if you can't hold a note! But you must be involved.

There is no such thing as the ministry of church attendance. Get involved either in your church or outside the church, but have a ministry.

Lastly, I love the fact that even a little faith can accomplish great things. Look what Jesus said in **Luke 17:6**, "If you have faith as a mustard seed, you can say to this mulberry tree, 'Be pulled up by the roots and be planted in the sea,' and it would obey you."

About The Author

David Garcia, Th.D., is the Lead Pastor of one of central Florida's most exciting churches, *Grace World Outreach Church*, located in Brooksville, Florida since May, 1998. For 40 years, Pastor Garcia has been blessed with unique insights into God's Word and an exceptional preach-teach style of presenting it. He possesses a prophetic gifting that speaks directly to the heart of the listener or reader. His anointing flows in evangelism with signs and wonders confirming the Word.

Pastor Garcia is a versatile and popular seminar, crusade, and conference speaker who offers a wealth of Biblical and practical ideas. He is also a gifted author of numerous books with a unique style of relevant presentation. He is also well known as a compassionate and balanced pastor.

David also travels nationally and internationally and serves as an advisor and spiritual father to ministries in the Philippines, Mexico, Tanzania, and several to pastors in the United States.

In 1974, David had a miraculous salvation experience in a hotel room, and later found God's call as a missionary in New York City and Zimbabwe, Africa. David and his wife, Nellie, have been married for 45 years and have two happily married children, both serving God in full-time ministry, and four wonderful grandchildren.

ENDNOTES

[1] Guillermo Maldonado, *The Kingdom of Power* (Whitaker House, New Kensington, PA, 2013)

[2] Myles Munroe, *Rediscovering the Kingdom* (Destiny Image Publishing, Shippensburg, PA, 2004)

[3] Bill Johnson, *When Heaven Invades Earth* (Destiny Image Publications, Shippensburg, PA, 2003)

[4] Maldonado, *The Kingdom of Power*, p.15

[5] Johnson, *When Heaven Invades Earth*, p. 58

[6] Munroe, *Rediscovering the Kingdom*, 158

[7] Maldonado, *The Kingdom of Power*, p. 28

[8] Munroe, *Rediscovering the Kingdom*, p. 159

[9] Ibid., p. 152

[10] Ibid., p. 155

[11] Ibid., p. 65

[12] Ibid., p. 65

[13] Ibid., p. 65

[14] John Bevere with Lee Bozeman, Larry Keefauver, and Neil Wilson, *Under Cover: The Promise of Protection Under His Authority: Leader's Guide* (W Publishing, a Thomas Nelson Company, Nashville, TN 2001) p.2

[15] Maldonado, *The Kingdom of Power*, p. 15

[16] Ibid., p.15

[17] Ibid., p. 25

[18] Ibid., p. 25

[19] John Bevere, *The Fear of the Lord* (Charisma House, Lake Mary, FL, 1997, 2006) pp39-60

[20] Maldonado, *The Kingdom of Power*, p. 65

[21] Ibid., p. 28

[22] S.D. Gordon, *Quiet Talks on Power* (Cosimo, Inc. Chelsea Station New York, NY, 1906) p.77

[23] Dina Temple—Raston and Steve Inskeep, NPR Sept. 29, 2015; www.npr.org, accesssed July 2016.

[24] "Dove's Eyes" by Rick Pino, from the CD titled *The Undiscovered*, 2008

[25] Maldonado, *The Kingdom of Power*, p. 114

[26] Gordon, *Quiet Talks on Power*, p. 77

[27] "Speaking of Animals." *Google Books*. N.p., n.d. Web. 26 Sept. 2016.

[28] Johnson, *When Heaven Invades Earth*, p. 62

[29] Ibid., p.39

[30] Bevere, *The Fear of the Lord*, p.77

If this book has been a blessing to you,
please let me know.

Pastor David Garcia

20366 Cortez Road

Brooksville, FL 34601

pastordavidgarcia@msn.com